The Resilient Clinician

The
Resilient
Clinician

ROBERT J. WICKS

OXFORD
UNIVERSITY PRESS
2008

OXFORD
UNIVERSITY PRESS

Oxford University Press, Inc., publishes works that further
Oxford University's objective of excellence
in research, scholarship, and education.

Oxford   New York
Auckland   Cape Town   Dar es Salaam   Hong Kong   Karachi
Kuala Lumpur   Madrid   Melbourne   Mexico City   Nairobi
New Delhi   Shanghai   Taipei   Toronto

With offices in
Argentina   Austria   Brazil   Chile   Czech Republic   France   Greece
Guatemala   Hungary   Italy   Japan   Poland   Portugal   Singapore
South Korea   Switzerland   Thailand   Turkey   Ukraine   Vietnam

Copyright © 2008 by Oxford University Press, Inc.

Published by Oxford University Press, Inc.
198 Madison Avenue, New York, New York 10016

www.oup.com

Oxford is a registered trademark of Oxford University Press

Portions of this book appeared earlier in *Overcoming Secondary Stress in
Medical and Nursing Practice: A Guide to Professional Resilience and
Personal Well-Being* (Oxford University Press, 2006).

All rights reserved. No part of this publication may be reproduced,
stored in a retrieval system, or transmitted, in any form or by any means,
electronic, mechanical, photocopying, recording, or otherwise,
without the prior permission of Oxford University Press.

Library of Congress Cataloging-in-Publication Data

Wicks, Robert J.
The resilient clinician / Robert J. Wicks.
p. ; cm.
Includes bibliographical references.
ISBN: 978-0-19-531697-1
1. Mental health personnel—Mental health. 2. Stress management.
I. Title. [DNLM: 1. Psychotherapy. 2. Counseling. 3. Health Personnel—
psychology. 4. Self Care. 5. Social Work. 6. Stress, Psychological—
therapy.   WM 420 W637r 2007]
RC451.4.P79W53 2007
616.89'14—dc22   2007013462

7 9 8

Printed in the United States of America
on acid-free paper

Following the devastation of Hurricane Katrina, the Veteran's Administration requested volunteers to assist in relief efforts in Louisiana, Mississippi, and Alabama. One of the many persons who stepped forward was a clinical social worker from a VA clinic in Wisconsin. With the encouragement of her husband, Peter, the enthusiasm of her little girls, Kaitlyn and Emily ("We're proud of you Mommy!"), and the support of her fine coworkers in Cleveland, Appleton, and Milwaukee, she went south to help, bringing her professionalism as well as her passion for providing support to veterans and their families.

This action was symbolic of the attitude of caring she had as a child and now—in a more mature way—she has as an adult. She is someone who truly carries on the wonderful heritage of her mother, who models compassion in so many touching ways. She is also the pride of her dad, who was proud of her as a child and is even more pleased at the woman she has become.

For my daughter Michaele W. Kulick, MSW, LCSW

Acknowledgments

Preparing a book like this requires a great deal of support from many different quarters. Sometimes a book is made possible by persons who believe in your work and provide the means by which you can take out the time to do the research and be able to share your work once it is done. For this assistance, I would like to thank Mary Catherine Bunting for her generosity and Judith Needham for her wise counsel.

Support also comes from within the educational setting in which you work. My chairperson, Joseph Ciarrocchi, as well as my deans, Amanda Thomas and Jim Buckley, offer all the assistance that is realistically possible in order to prepare well-researched publications for the profession. My graduate assistant, Stephanie Marinelli, also was a great support. She prevented me from being swamped by all the details that are part and parcel of a literature search and review of the final draft.

Guidance from the publisher is also a crucial determining factor in the quality of the gestalt of the book. Joan Bossert, Vice

Acknowledgments

President/Associate Publisher and Editorial Director at Oxford University Press in New York, is the type of editor professors truly need if their work is to be brought to its fullness. Her suggestion to incorporate material on positive psychology as it relates to the self-awareness process of clinicians and her enthusiasm about my inclusion of classic and recently published material on mindfulness clearly made this a better book.

Finally, all authors need both someone to inspire them and to provide editorial guidance as the manuscript is in process. I am lucky to have both gifts represented in the same person—my wife, Michaele Barry Wicks. If good comes from publication of this book, she certainly must take a lion's share of the credit.

Contents

Contents

Contents

The Resilient Clinician

Continually Creating New Inner Psychological Space

An Ongoing Process of Mindfulness

They may forget what you said but they will never forget how you made them feel.

—Carl W. Buechner

Sometimes a brief interchange with a patient may leave us speechless. One such instance for me happened at the end of a long course of psychotherapy with an adult client who was sexually abused as a child. As I began to ask a series of wrap-up questions, my goal was to elicit summative answers or paradigms she had learned that would provide internal guidance for her in the future. Then, when she entered darkness again—for darkness comes again and again for all who are self-aware and compassionate, as she was—she would know how to better handle it. I also wanted her to take credit for all the hard work she had done in therapy. At least those were my intentions. Her response to my intervention, though, would leave *me* with a lesson worth remembering.

To accomplish my goal, I waited until her voice was bubbling with confidence and joy. I then said, "Let's stop for a minute. Picture my face as a mirror; what do you see?"

She quickly responded, "I see a woman alive with *life*—a woman who has resurrected the child who was lost because of the abuse. She has also integrated her with the secure woman she is now and because of that, she is hot stuff!"

Her exuberance made us both laugh. Following this, I then asked, "Well, how did you get to this point? You weren't this way when you first came in to see me." My expectation was that in response she would review the approaches learned and healthy beliefs integrated in her life during the treatment. Instead, her face showed surprise, and she blurted out, "You mean, you don't know?"

"No. Not exactly," I replied.

"Well," she said, "it was simple."

"Simple?" I replied. (Now it was my turn to be surprised.)

"Yes. You see, the first time I came in here to see you, I simply watched how you sat with me; then I began sitting with myself in the same way."

This is the healing space we hope to offer others in therapy, but naturally we don't always succeed. It is also a milieu not just confined to the consulting room or the behavioral science professions. Though different words may be used to describe it, this special sense of presence is something all persons in the helping and healing professions need to be able to offer others so that they may see the possibility of change.

For instance, once when Nobel Peace Prize winner Archbishop Desmond Tutu of South Africa was speaking at General

Theological Seminary in New York City, one of the students sitting in the audience nudged the dean, who was sitting next to him, and whispered, "Desmond Tutu is a holy man." The dean in response asked, "How do you really know this?" To which the young man quickly replied, "I know that Desmond Tutu is holy because when I'm with him *I* feel holy."

The above two experiences, first by a sexually abused client and then by a seminarian listening to a well-known minister and social justice activist, raise two challenging questions for all working in the helping or healing professions. The first is: What do people experience when they are with us? Do they experience a sense of respectful space where they can rest their burdens, anger, questions, projections, stress, anxiety, and wonder? Or, do they feel our sense of exhaustion, need to always be right or in control, or even our desire to be viewed as wise, attractive, witty, or helpful? What do people feel when they are with us? This is an important question that we must reflect upon during the sessions and the times between them for the sake of ourselves as well as those we serve.

As psychologist, meditation teacher, and author Jack Kornfield recognizes:

> The understanding of emptiness is contagious: It appears we can catch it from one another. We know that when a sad or angry person enters a room, we too often enter into sadness or anger. It shouldn't surprise us, then, that the presence of a teacher who is empty, open, awake can have a powerful effect on another person, especially if that person is ripe. (2000, p. 79)

Therapist Jeffrey Kottler offers a parallel comment in his classic work *On Being a Therapist*:

> The first and foremost element of change, then, is the therapist's presence—his excitement, enthusiasm, and the power of his personality.... The therapist enters the relationship with clarity, openness, and serenity and comes fully prepared to encounter a soul in torment. The client comes prepared with his own expectations for a mentor, a guru, a doctor, a friend, or a wizard. (1989, p. 3)

In keeping with this line of thinking, Brazier points out as well in his intriguing book *Zen Therapy*:

> The safe space of therapy depends upon the therapists' inner calm.... Tranquility erodes the mind's conditioning. Conditioning makes us compulsive.... The person whose life is governed by "I could not possibly ..." "I must never ..." "I always have to ..." and so on is not free and feels inwardly oppressed. (1954/1995, p. 54)

This leads us to a second interrelated question (and the one of greater import for us in this book), namely:

> Are we able to sit with *ourselves* in the same way that we wish to be with the clients or patients who turn to us for help?

In other words, do we also have a deep sense of respect and intrigue about our own cognitions (e.g., ways of perceiving, thinking, and understanding), affect, and behavior? Can we maintain the same fine balance between clarity and kindness with ourselves that we try to offer to our clients? Put another way: Can we be honest and caring with, and of, ourselves so we can continue to learn each day what it means to be both an effective helper and be able to live as mindfully and completely as possible in all aspects of our life?

Answering these questions has an impact both on the clinician and the persons who seek the clinician's help. And so, this is a strong added impetus for self-awareness and self-care for those in the healing and helping professions. To quote Kottler once again:

> The practice of psychotherapy permits a unique life-style in which one's personal and professional roles complement each other . . . all our personal experience, our travels, learning, conversations, reading or intimate dealing with life's joys and sorrows provide the foundation for everything we do in our therapy sessions. . . . The decision to improve the mental health of others is a choice to improve *ourselves* in the process. (1989, p. 28, italics added)

STRUCTURE OF THE BOOK

So, given the above two questions, the essence of this book is concerned with how we as clinicians care for and know ourselves so we continually have the "space" to offer others. These interrelated objectives will be addressed through an exploration of possible approaches to:

- Identifying and reviewing the dangers of denial;
- Being aware of the ongoing challenges of acute and chronic secondary stress;

- Improving the quality of one's self-care protocol;
- Sensitizing clinicians to the place of mindfulness and meditation in the daily routine of the therapist, counselor, and social worker;
- Increasing the awareness of our gifts as clinicians while becoming more intrigued with, rather than burdened by, our growing edges as persons and professionals given the recent contributions of positive psychology and Zen therapy/contemporary Buddhist psychology; and finally by
- Appreciating the joys, nobility, and privilege of being a clinician in such challenging times.

In order to enhance the flow of this book, when exploring these topics, most of the material that would normally be included as tables in the body of the text has been presented as appendixes at the end of the text. In addition, given the clinician's often very demanding schedule, this book is intentionally quite brief. It can be read through in a single sitting to circumvent the resistance sometimes present when confronted with "yet another lengthy work to read." (For further reading in those areas touched upon that prove to be of special interest to the reader, though, both selected and general bibliographies are included.)

The overarching goal of this work, then, is to introduce and highlight those areas that can help renew clinicians in today's challenging climate. It is amazing how little it can take to change the emotional tide in favor of such a beneficial move. Small alterations in behavior can sometimes jumpstart a positive step to a healthier attitude more than disputing our dysfunctional thoughts ever can. For instance, shortly after graduating from Hahnemann Medical College with my doctorate in psychology, I dove into a sea of work, as new graduates often do. I was teaching full-time at Bryn Mawr College's Graduate School of Social Work and Social Research, developed a counseling load of 15–20 patients weekly, consulted, did clinical research, wrote . . . and quickly became emotionally exhausted!

Despite all of this work, though, I decided to accept "just one more invitation" to speak to a group of educators on, of all topics, "burnout." As I prepared for the talk, I thought, "What a charlatan. I'm fatigued myself, and I, of all people, am going to address this topic?" However, an unusual thing happened when I started reading the recent clinical papers and research findings published on burnout, or what is sometimes now referred to as "compassion fatigue." Surprising to me, rather than my absorption in the clinical and research material on the topic draining me further, I felt more and more exhilarated by what I read.

I could now not only label the problem but also frame an approach both to facing the toxic work stress I was experiencing and to improving the overall quality of my personal life. Also, when I brought this information and the increased energy I felt to the informal self-debriefing I normally undertook each day as a carry-over from my early clinical training, I also could see that I was reinvesting myself again in the wonders of the profession. I was beginning to recall my original love for the challenges of the clinical field rather than mindlessly and compulsively moving from task to task. Moreover, I found myself appreciating and seeking to enhance the signature gifts and talents supervisors had pointed out in me instead of merely focusing on the shortcomings and "countertransferences" I noticed. This epiphany has never totally left me and has been reinforced most recently by the material published on mindfulness, positive psychology, and Zen therapy/Buddhist psychology. It is also the source of the spirit in which I offer this brief book.

The Resilient Clinician is structured and written so that in one sitting clinicians can begin to frame both the questions about and approaches to limiting secondary stress and improving the quality of their lives in a positive, hopeful, yet quite practical way. The question that is always before all of us as clinicians is:

> What do I need to put into place in my own life that will enable me to reap the most out of having the privilege to participate in such a noble profession and, in turn, experience a more meaningful personal life in the process?

Reading and reviewing the following chapters and appendixes are designed to spur action to address this question. Not to expend such energy is at the most basic level impractical. Given the delicate nature of the work clinicians do, avoiding the application of simple principles on limiting secondary stress, enhancing one's own self-care protocol, increasing a sense of mindfulness, and incorporating positive psychology in one's own life is potentially dangerous for us as well as for those we treat. Yet, as strange as it may sound, many of us still opt to do this at times. As Kottler and Hazler (1997) note, there are oft-spoken rationalizations for avoidance of facing our own challenges. All of us have heard or spoken such statements as:

- "This period will pass. I am just busier at this point."
- "I'm an experienced clinician who knows how to keep stress in his private life out of his work."

- "None of my colleagues or clients have complained to me about my not being 100% effective as a clinician."
- "I'm a clinician with great skills, so I can deal with this difficulty without any input from others."

DENIAL

If there is an apt proverb for the articulated and unspoken demands many people make of psychotherapists, counselors, and social workers, it surely must be the Yiddish one: "Sleep faster. We need the pillows!" Furthermore, in addition to the unrealistic expectations they face, the stakes are now extremely high for professionals in mental health and social work. The potential for developing such psychological problems as emotional blunting at one end of the spectrum or extreme affectivity at the other are quite great. Many of us deny personal emotional needs as a survival mechanism. However, clinicians who follow the implicit advice to protect themselves by not allowing themselves to feel too much emotion, sympathy, or sadness run the risk of shutting down entirely in the process and losing the joy and empathy that are so necessary for being a clinician who can thrive and be a true healing presence to others.

Pope and Vasquez, in their book *How to Survive and Thrive as a Therapist*, note some potentially negative consequences when clinicians ignore stress and neglect self-care. They include:

Disrespecting Work: Therapists who become depleted and discouraged through a lack of self-care may begin trivializing, ridiculing, or becoming overly self-critical about what they do. . . . **Making More Mistakes:** . . . Monitoring, acknowledging, accepting responsibility for, and attempting to address the consequences of our mistakes is one of our fundamental responsibilities. . . . But self-neglect can lead to impaired ability to attend to work. . . . We find ourselves scheduling two clients at the same time, forgetting to show up for an appointment, calling a client by the wrong name, misplacing a client's chart, or locking ourselves out of our own office. . . . **Lacking Energy:** They may wake up tired . . . fight to stay awake and alert during a session, wonder how they're ever going to make it through the rest of the work day. . . . **Using Work to Block Out Unhappiness, Pain and Discontent:** More and more clients, projects, and responsibilities are taken on until little if any free time is available to reflect on our lives, to spend time alone apart from work, or to become aware of how empty, demoralized, or miserable we are. . . . **Losing Interest:** We no longer feel the investment in the work and the connection to our clients. . . . Lack of self-care can lead to a lack of caring. (2005, pp. 14–15)

Professionals seem so discouraged at times that they don't even consider—given the culture and their own personal resources—that there are possible practical approaches to deal with environmental and intrapersonal sources of stress in mental health and social work settings. Instead, unfortunately, they just march on. When I had a session with one very competent counselor who was starting to manifest early symptoms of chronic secondary stress such as hypersensitivity, increased daily use of alcohol, and sleep disturbance, I asked him how he would characterize his own problem. He said, "I may not be burned out yet." Then, after a brief pause, he smiled slightly and added, "But I think I'm experiencing at least a 'brown out'!"

Acknowledging his insight, I asked that given the precarious situation he recognized himself in, what type of self-care protocol did he design and employ for himself to prevent further deterioration of his emotional well-being? In response, after sighing, he said, "I only wish I had the time for something like that!"

Time, of course, is so limited for clinicians. More and more I am aware of this even in my own life. Shortly after I received my doctorate from Hahnemann Medical College, a physician who had one of the busiest practices in the area came in for an initial psychological assessment. He was having an extramarital affair. Being a new graduate, I remember carefully formulating a Freudian theoretical diagnosis in my mind. If he were to come in to see me now, though, I must confess that I think my first unspoken reaction would be: "Where does he get the time?" For mental health and social work professionals, time is especially precious. In response, they need to schedule their priorities and ensure that what they do is accomplished in the most effective way possible.

Persons in the medical and nursing professions realize that "for every poisoned worker there are a dozen with sub-clinical toxicity" (Scott & Hawk, 1986, p. ix). Using this as a metaphor for the problem of secondary stress, clinicians also need to realize that for every case of serious psychological impairment, there are many professional caregivers who are starting to manifest some of the symptoms of chronic or acute secondary stress but may not even realize it until well after the fact. Since this is so, I believe a clinically sound approach is not just to be proactive by addressing the dangers involved in mental health and social work but also to uncover the ways that those very challenges can be channeled to help persons become deeper because of them.

As was mentioned earlier, the most insidious danger to clinicians is denial. Fortunately, this factor practically atrophies of its own accord once we accept the following simple reality:

The seeds of secondary stress and the seeds of true passionate involvement in the fields of counseling, psychology, and social work are actually the *same* seeds.

Once again, the question is *not* whether stress will appear and take a toll on those working as clinicians. Instead, it is to what extent professionals take the essential steps to appreciate, limit, and learn from this very stress to continue—and even deepen—their personal lives and roles as helpers and healers.

There are so many stresses not only in clinical practice but also in the personal lives of those whose work is to help others. A difficult marriage, raising adolescents, physical illness, financial pressures, loss of loved ones—sometimes the list seems endless. Complicating these problems further is that the apparent solutions suggested seem to be unrealistic as well. In most continuing education (CEU) programs for counselors, social workers, and psychotherapists, stress prevention courses are offered. However, when a list of the problems caregivers must face is presented and reviewed, the oft-heard "back of the room" response by those attending is: "Yes, I knew that all along. So what? There's nothing you can do about it. It is part of the territory of being a clinician." Then, when a long list of stress reducers is subsequently offered, unconsciously the response to that may also be to put these recommendations in a "mental draw" marked: "Nice if I had the time or energy but totally unrealistic given the myriad demands of my schedule." And, to some extent this may well be true. After all, to be honest, who has the time for half of what is suggested in these workshops? (As a matter of fact, even pondering doing some of these involved, time-consuming stress-reduction steps offered may become stressful!)

On the other hand, denying the dangers posed by secondary stress as well as resisting a reasonable process of self-knowledge and self-care under the guise that it, too, is impractical is an attitude to be avoided at all costs. Given this distinction between a reasonable and unrealistic self-care process, the premise of this book is tied to a significantly different question from the one just posed above. It is not: "Who has the time to follow this long list of suggestions?" Instead, it is: "Who in their right mind would not take out the time to ponder the *essentials* of self-knowledge, self-care, and secondary stress?"

The practical steps to achieving a new perspective and maintaining self-care are actually quite simple, though they are not always easy due to the clinicians' well-entrenched habits and current workloads. However, these two logjams of resistance can be dealt with in an incremental way by reading the brief treatment of secondary stress, self-care, mindfulness, and positive psychology presented in this book with an eye to seeing new possibilities and then acting upon them *in some initial way*. That, in reality, is neither impossible nor unrealistic. Moreover, isn't a sense of openness to new insights and taking initial actions in a healthier direction actually what we expect of our clients? Why, then, should we not expect the same of ourselves?

CHAPTER ONE

Sensing the Dangers

Chronic and Acute
Secondary Stress

Generally, research . . . suggests that burnout, once
it occurs, can lead to a host of therapeutic mistakes.
It can be difficult to recover from. Thus, it seems
important to prevent burnout rather than wait for it
to occur and then try to remediate it.

> —Marsha Linehan, *Cognitive-Behavioral*
> *Treatment of Borderline Personality Disorder*

Do not believe that he who seeks to comfort you lives
untroubled among the simple and quiet words that
sometimes do you good. His life has much difficulty
and sadness and remains far behind yours. Were
it otherwise he would never have been able to find
those words.

> —Rainer Maria Rilke, *Letters to a Young Poet*

Calm seas do not make skillful sailors.

> —African proverb

There is no getting around the stresses associated with being a clinician. In many cases, it is also not possible to remove them. Instead, facing them is like tacking through rough waters. In his book *First You Have to Row a Little Boat*, Richard Bode describes this approach quite well:

> To tack a boat, to sail a zigzag course, is not to deny our destination or our destiny—despite how it may appear to those who never dare to take the tiller in their hand. Just the opposite: It's to recognize the obstacles that stand between ourselves and where we want to go, and then to maneuver with patience and fortitude, making the most of each leg of our journey, until we reach our landfall. (1993, p. 49)

To my mind, "tacking" is an ideal metaphor for the way clinicians must face pressures in general, and chronic and acute secondary stress in particular, in the field of mental health today. To ignore what must be faced or simply seek to take everything head on may be disastrous both personally and professionally. On the other hand, knowledge and maturity help us to psychologically tack the stressful waters that must be encountered at times so we can make the most of all that we face as caregivers. Such navigation must include a basic appreciation of the elements of both chronic and acute secondary stress.

CHRONIC SECONDARY STRESS

Russian playwright Anton Chekhov once proclaimed: "Any idiot can face a crisis—it's this day-to-day living that wears you out"

(Chekhov, source unknown). As the psychiatrist in the novel *The Case of Lucy Bending* laments in a way that rings all too true as a danger for all clinicians in real life:

> Most laymen, he supposed, believed psychiatrists fell apart under the weight of other people's problems. Dr. Theodore Levin had another theory. He feared that a psychiatrist's life force gradually leaked out. It was expended on sympathy, understanding, and the obsessive need to heal and help create whole lives. Other people's lives. But always from the outside. Always the observer. Then one day he would wake up and discover that he himself was empty, drained. (Sanders, 1982, p. 42)

The problem for many of us doing clinical work is that the causes of burnout are often so quiet and insidious that we fail to notice them until they have caused a great deal of harm. Communication theorist Marshall McLuhan once posed the question: "If the temperature of the bath rises one degree every ten minutes, how will the bather know when to scream?" (McLuhan, source unknown). Today, the demands of private practice, the threat of lawsuits, financial needs, a psychologically toxic institutional/clinical environment are but a few of the pressures clinicians must face.

To my mind, no one has written more eloquently and convincingly throughout his entire professional career on the challenges and joys of being a clinician than Jeffrey Kottler has. In his classic work *On Being a Therapist*, for instance, some of his more pertinent observations are:

- To take on a client, any client, is to make a tremendous commitment to that person that could last years if not a lifetime. . . . It will have moments of special closeness and times of great hardship. The client will, at times, worship you, scorn you, abuse you, play with you, and want to devour you. And through it all, regardless of what is going on in your own life—sickness, births, deaths, joys, disappointment—you must be there for the client, always waiting. (1989, p. 8)

- Let us not pretend it does not hurt when a client abruptly ends treatment. . . . Clearly, we can make up some excuse about "primitive defenses" or "resistance" that we may even believe, and maybe the referral source will buy it, but deep, deep inside is a quiet little voice that will say: "You blew it." If such an episode occurs in the same week in which we have a few too many cancellations we are well on our way to a major bout of self-doubt. (p. 11)
- The principal hazard of our profession is the narcissistic belief that we are really special. . . . When we direct the interacting, questioning, controlling, confronting, nurturing, and even summarize at appropriate intervals for eight hours a day, it is an abrupt shock to our system to find ourselves at home or with friends struggling to be heard like everyone else. (p. 17)

These points, the myriad of other factors, and the negative self-talk all clinicians become prey to at times make it imperative that we have a greater understanding of chronic secondary stress (burnout, compassion fatigue) if self-understanding and self-care are to become an ongoing reality in our work as clinicians. As a result, a quick summary of "burnout" and then acute secondary stress (or vicarious PTSD) would be beneficial before focusing on: the development of a self-care protocol, the potential helpful role of including mindfulness techniques in one's daily routine, and examining the process of self-awareness—given the recent contributions of positive psychology—in enhancing resiliency in the clinician.

DEFINITION AND CAUSES OF BURNOUT

Edelwich and Brodsky, in one of the first academic book-length treatments of the topic of burnout, defined it as a "progressive loss of idealism, energy, and purpose experienced by people in the helping professions" (1980, p. 14). Freudenberger, who coined the term "burnout," described it as "a depletion or exhaustion of a person's mental and physical resources attributed to his or her prolonged, yet unsuccessful striving toward unrealistic expectations, internally or externally derived" (Keller & Ritt, 1984, p. 223).

Since Freudenberger introduced this term, the necessity of a unique concept of burnout has been questioned since the same symptoms and signs are seen in other disorders (depression, anxiety). So, when referring to burnout and the interventions needed to prevent or limit it, some professionals feel it is confusing the issue unnecessarily. However, many in the field, including myself, feel that the term is still quite helpful. If nothing else, the term "burnout" implicitly recognizes it is "legitimate" for persons in the healing and helping professions to experience stress, anxiety, depression, and other negative feelings. Moreover, it provides an integrated way to look at the emotional stress clinicians experience in their work.

The causes for burnout are legion. As Pfifferling helps us to appreciate, trying to pin down one source of burnout is futile. "As with diseases or conditions that do not have a single cause, there are multiple suggestions as to the origin, contributing factors, and types of susceptible hosts" (Pfifferling, 1986, p. 3).

Psychiatrist James Gill, in an article on the topic, wryly notes that "helping people can be extremely hazardous to your physical and mental health." He then goes on to indicate those clinicians who are good candidates for burnout:

Judging from the research done in recent years, along with clinical experience, it appears that those who fall into the following categories are generally the most vulnerable: (1) those who work exclusively with distressed persons; (2) those who work intensively with demanding people who feel entitled to assistance in solving their . . . problems; (3) those who are charged with the responsibility for too many individuals; (4) those who feel strongly motivated to work with people but who are prevented from doing so by too many administrative paper work tasks; (5) those who have an inordinate need to save people from their undesirable situations but find the task impossible; (6) those who are very perfectionistic and thereby invite failure; (7) those who feel guilty about their own human needs (which, if met, would enable them to serve others with stamina, endurance and emotional equanimity); (8) those who are too idealistic in their aims; (9) those whose personality is such that they need to champion underdogs; (10) those who cannot tolerate variety, novelty, or diversion in their work life; and (11) those who lack criteria for measuring the success of their undertakings but who experience an intense need to know that they are doing a good job. (1980, pp. 24–25)

Most researchers and authors on the topic of burnout (including me—see appendix A) have developed their own tailored list of the causes of burnout. And, as I have pointed out elsewhere:

There is much overlap, though, and all of them seem to point to the problem as being a *lack* which produces frustration. It can be a deficiency of such things as: education, opportunity, free time, ability, chance to ventilate, institutional power, variety, meaningful tasks, criteria to measure impact, coping mechanisms, staff harmony, professional and personal recognition, insight into one's motivations, balance in one's schedule, and emotional distance from the client population. . . . Since the factors on the above list are present to some degree in every human services setting, the potential for burnout is always present. (Wicks, 2003, p. 336)

Consequently, every healing professional is in danger of impairment in some way *to some extent*. Unfortunately, though, care is usually provided in most settings only to those professionals seriously enough impaired to be required by their state boards to seek out help. Furthermore, it is very difficult for many clinicians to admit to difficulties when they haven't reached crisis proportions—and even at that point some still deny problems. As W. H. Auden aptly noted, "Conscious insensitivity is a self-contradiction" (Auden, 1976, p. ix).

As a result, even though the topic of chronic secondary stress in not a new or novel one, unfortunately, the danger of burnout still exists as a serious threat to the psychological welfare of mental health and social work professionals and, in turn, those they serve, making greater awareness of the presentation, causes, and description of compassion fatigue, or burnout, quite necessary. Too often we hear the following statements by counselors, social workers, and psychotherapists and then take them as part of clinical and social work "territory" (especially in the often toxic institutional settings) rather than as symptoms that require response and further vigilance:

- *Cynicism*: "I just see this as a job. Being a therapist is not what it used to be. Nothing is going to change. People also ask me such trivial questions and burden me with stupid things."
- *Workaholism*: "I need to constantly check my email and phone mail even when I am not working on the weekend." "My husband and I need to earn a down payment for a house so I have to work more shifts than I'd like."
- *Isolation*: "I really don't feel part of things on the unit. The other staff members are nice people but I feel so different and isolated from them. I never discuss my work or personal life with any of them."
- *Boredom*: "I am so tired of doing the same thing every day. When I'm not killing myself, I'm bored to tears. If I hadn't so much invested in this field already, I would get out. I can't wait until the end of a shift."
- *Depletion*: "I feel it is taking me longer and longer to do less and less. I no longer feel the passion about the job as I did in the past. I am tired before I begin.

I don't quite dread going into work but it certainly is getting to that point. All I think about is the job."

- *Conflict*: "Everything seems to get on my nerves now. I fight with the patients, am irritable with the other staff, and am no fun to be with at home. I also resent having to deal with patients' families and feel that people are asking too much from me."

- *Arrogance*: "I wish I didn't have to deal with such incompetent co-workers. Also, I wish the patients would just follow what I tell them to do. One even had the nerve to ask for a referral to another therapist when I told her my diagnosis and treatment plan."

- *Helplessness:* "I am not sure I really can do anything to change my situation. This is the workload I have to deal with plain and simple. Also, my sleeping is often disturbed, I have no time for family and friends, my sinuses are always bothering me, and I know I drink too much coffee in the morning and too much wine in the evening." (Wicks, 2006, pp. 24–25)

So professionals in social work and mental health, rather than simply avoiding the dangers of burnout (as good as this may be), should also take clear steps to prevent acceleration of stress that is endemic to private and institutional clinical practice. To do this, it is important to appreciate the levels of burnout and to take out time to identify potential problem areas and review how they are being addressed. Developing a self-tailored *Clinicians' Vulnerability Profile* is a key resource for avoiding the hazards of insidious burnout.

LEVELS OF BURNOUT

The symptoms of chronic secondary stress include: frustration, depression, apathy, helplessness, impatience, disengagement, emotional depletion, cynicism, hopelessness, a significant decline in one's professional self-esteem and confidence, feeling overwhelmed and anhedonia (Wicks, 2003; Skovholt, 2001; Maslach & Jackson, 1981; Gill, 1980; Baker, 2003). However, for our purposes here, it may be helpful to break down the possible progression of burnout for illustrative purposes, even though there is significant overlap between the levels of burnout.

Among the ways burnout has been broken down, the levels provided by psychiatrist James Gill appear to be most helpful for clinicians:

> The *first level* is characterized by signs and symptoms that are relatively mild, short in duration and occur only occasionally [see appendix B]. . . . The *second level* is reached when signs and symptoms have become *more stable, last longer* and are *tougher* to get rid of. . . . The *third level* is experienced when signs and symptoms have become *chronic* and a *physical illness* has developed. (1980, pp. 22–23, italics added)

As I have explained elsewhere, this

commonsense breakdown is very much in line with the medical model and there is some overlap between levels. While they could be applied to any physical or psychological constellation of symptoms and signs, they provide a reasonable way of delineating a breakdown of the burnout syndrome. The third level is self-explanatory. And in line with what is known about serious prolonged countertransference [feelings on the helpers' part toward patients and colleagues that have sources in their own past] . . . the signs, symptoms, and treatment are obvious. . . . If the [caregiver] is experiencing a life crisis and undergoing notable ongoing psychosomatic problems, then it means that preventive measures and self-administered treatments have failed. Psychological and medical assistance is necessary. This may mean entering or re-entering psycho-therapy and obtaining, as advised by the therapist, medical help if necessary. Once this third level has been reached, the burnout is severe and remediation of the problem will likely take a good deal of time and effort. (Wicks, 2003, p. 37)

This is why preventative measures before reaching a point that we are referring to here as "level 3" is essential. Since the seeds of burn-out and the seeds of enthusiasm are in reality the same seeds, anyone who truly cares can expect that they will need to ride the waves of burnout—and occasionally get knocked down by a wave they missed! Basic steps in averting burnout (see appendix C) should, in most cases, prevent many of the difficulties. Level 2 means:

where the burnout problem has become more severe and intractable to brief interventions, a more profound effort is necessary. [See appendix D.] Central to such actions is a willingness to reorient priorities and take risks with one's style of dealing with the world, which for some reason is not working optimally. To accomplish this, frequently one's colleagues . . . [and] mentor need to become involved. Their support and insight for dealing with the distress being felt is needed. The uncomfortable steps taken to unlock oneself from social problems and the temptation to deal with them in a single unproductive way (repetition compulsion) requires all of the guidance and support one can obtain. In many cases, this also requires a break from work for a vacation or retreat in order to distance oneself from the work for a time so that revitalization and reorientation can occur. (Wicks, 2003, p. 338)

All clinicians experience level 1 burnout at times throughout the year. It is part of the ups and downs of being in an intense profession. Most helping professionals also experience level 2 burnout at times and some unfortunately level 3. This is why awareness of the ever present challenges of stress, being as self-aware as possible, utilizing this self-knowledge, developing a self-care protocol, and knowing the benefits of mindfulness are all essential. Beyond this, if we face stress constructively, not only do we lessen the chances of it turning into extreme distress, but we also are in a position to learn from it in a way that deepens us. However, this requires both the right type of knowledge and the humility to turn to others for help when we don't progress as we should—not an easy task when people often assume that because we are in the mental health and social work fields, we are omnipotent, always strong, and usually right.

The reality, however, is far from the projections people put onto us. We all have personalities-in-process, growing edges, and are vulnerable to certain stresses, situations, and patient/colleague personality types. As a result, it would help immeasurably for us to be aware, through self-questioning, of where these vulnerable points are so we are not caught unawares.

CLINICIANS' VULNERABILITY PROFILE

Knowing what types of people and problems give you difficulty is the first step toward avoiding psychological vulnerability. Given this knowledge, no matter how experienced the clinician may be, the following simple questions (questionnaire 1.1) may provide an avenue to helpful information with respect to individual stress points that they may experience.

By addressing questions like these honestly and completely, you can begin to see the areas where you have progressed and developed effective coping skills. Other areas will need attention—sometimes *constant* attention—given our ingrained personality style. To ignore these areas is to court unnecessary stress. Even when you yourself don't feel the stress, this can translate into a problem. As one professional told me when I questioned him about his problems with stress, "I don't think I really am usually under stress, but I think I'm a carrier!" When we do induce stress in others, they, in turn, make life difficult for other workers, family, etc., and this creates burnout contagion, which will eventually come back to haunt the "carrier" and decrease efficiency in the organization. That is why it is good to have some familiarity with the approaches necessary to lessen the stress in those around us even if we may not be experiencing it ourselves.

ACUTE SECONDARY STRESS: VICARIOUS PTSD

Psychologist Jeffrey Kottler said about the threats to his personal sense of well-being that were a byproduct of his work as a therapist: "Never mind that we catch our clients' colds and flus, what about their pessimism, negativity. . . . Words creep back to haunt us. Those silent screams remain deafening" (Kottler, 1989, p. 8). What he is obviously speaking about here is the destabilization of one's own personality as a result of constant treatment of the severe psychological, physical, and sexual trauma experienced by others.

Vicarious Post Traumatic Stress Disorder is a great danger today (Herman, 1997; Linehan, 1993). Increasingly clinicians are called upon to ease the suffering patients are experiencing due to the psychic trauma that arises from physical, psychological, and spiritual abuse, rape, as well as other physical assaults, and terrorism. When this mixes with the stress clinicians experience in their own lives—including marital, financial, personal, and world instability—the result is quite psychologically toxic. Unrecognized it could lead to severe impairment or a psychological "grayness" in how clinicians may experience their lives, as well as a resultant inadequate treatment of their clients due to their unrecognized/unaccepted impaired emotional state.

One of the most sensible approaches to recognizing, limiting, avoiding, and even learning from the onset of vicarious PTSD is to conduct daily debriefings with yourself. A second approach is to have an organized way to question yourself to uncover the presence and/or duration of clusters of PTSD signs and symptoms. These two approaches go hand in hand. As I have noted previously:

> Persons in the helping professions . . . at times lose distance and are temporarily swept away by the expectations, needs, painful experiences, and negativity of others. More than most people, they are confronted with negativity and sadness. Yet, they are educated to pick up these signs as early as possible so they are not unnecessarily dragged down. We can

learn much from how they avoid losing perspective or regain it when they temporarily lose their way. The distance they value can help us deal with the pain of others.

There is much to remembering the Russian proverb: "When you live next to the cemetery, you can't cry for everyone who dies." Most of us, whether we are professional helpers or not, tend to personalize too much. We absorb the sadness, anxiety, and negativity of those around us. Sometimes we even feel this is expected of us. . . . As we listen to stories of terrible things that happen [or observe them] . . . we catch some of their futility, fear, vulnerability, and hopelessness rather than experiencing mere frustration or concern. We learn that no matter how professionally prepared we are, we are not immune to the psychological and spiritual dangers that arise in living a full life of involvement with others. I remember learning this the hard way myself.

In 1994 I did a psychological debriefing of some of the relief workers evacuated from Rwanda's bloody civil war. I interviewed each person and gave them an opportunity to tell their stories. As they related the horrors they had experienced, they seemed to be grateful for an opportunity to ventilate. They recounted the details again and again, relating their feelings as well as descriptions of the events which triggered them. Their sense of futility, their feelings of guilt, their sense of alienation, their experiences with emotional outbursts, all came to the fore.

In addition to listening, I gave them handouts on what to possibly expect down the road (problems sleeping, difficulties trusting and relating to others, flashbacks and the like). As I moved through the process of debriefing and providing information so they could have a frame of reference for understanding their experiences, I thought to myself, "This is going pretty well." Then, something happened that shifted my whole experience.

In the course of one of the final interviews, one of the relief workers related stories of how certain members of the Hutu tribe raped and dismembered their Tutsi foes. Soon, I noticed I was holding onto my chair for dear life. I was doing what some young people call "white knuckling it."

After the session, I did what I usually do after an intense encounter . . . a countertransferential review. (If time doesn't permit then, I do it at the end of the day—every day.) In doing this, I get in touch with my feelings by asking myself: What made me sad? Overwhelmed me? Sexually aroused me? Made me extremely happy or even confused me? Being brutally honest with myself, I try to put my finger on the pulse of my emotions.

The first thing that struck me about this particular session was the tight grip I had on the chair as the session with the relief worker progressed. "What was I feeling when I did this? Why did I do this?"

It didn't take me long to realize that their terrible stories had broken through my defenses and normal sense of distance and detachment. I was holding onto the chair because quite simply, I was frightened to death that if I didn't I would be pulled into the vortex of darkness myself.

That recognition alone helped lessen the pain and my fearful uneasiness. I then proceeded with a . . . countertransferential review . . . used by therapists . . . to prevent the slide into unnecessary darkness and to learn—and thus benefit—from the events for the day. (Wicks, 2002, pp. 54–56, 109)

The questions we can ask ourselves to determine whether vicarious PTSD may well be present are fairly straightforward since they are in line with the questions we would ask our own clients who were demonstrating the results of a traumatic encounter. (See questionnaire 1.2.)

The essential frame of reference to use in understanding this self-questioning is that having these symptoms is no more a sign of personal weakness than having the symptoms of any psychological or medical disorder. This is important to note at the outset so self-blame, self-debasement, or bravado does not prevent a careful self-examination—especially after a particularly difficult client/clinical encounter. Working with young victims of sexual abuse, pediatric oncology patients, severe borderline clients, cases of brutal rape or other physical/emotional violence over a period of time would take a toll on anyone.

To ensure that clinicians consider this self-reflection approach, I point them to the following general principles to keep in mind when seeking self-understanding following a single or series of traumatic encounters. (Although therapists, social workers, and counselors might provide similar guidelines to their clients, I have found that in more instances than one might expect, clinicians did not use ones like them in their own self-debriefing when dealing extensively with persons with PTSD.) Such guidelines might include the simple suggestions to:

1. Be as nonjudgmental and accepting of yourself as you would in dealing with those you treat who have undergone a traumatic event;
2. Constantly remember that the symptoms you are experiencing as a result of the traumatic encounter(s) are

related to the experience(s) itself rather than to an inherent personality weakness or lack of personality strength in oneself;

3. Know that when you are dealing with trauma on an ongoing basis as part of the work you do, then dealing with the symptoms and dangers of vicarious PTSD on an ongoing basis—rather than as a once and for all event—is to be expected; and

4. Share your feelings and concerns with others. It is clinically wise; those who seek to go it alone either wind up leaving the field or acting out in unhealthy ways (e.g. alcoholism, overdetachment, promiscuity, etc.).

Although we hear a lot about PTSD today—especially after the September 11 attacks on the World Trade Center and the Pentagon—as clinicians well know, it is far from a new phenomenon. Given this, the following succinct summary (according to Foy, Drescher, Fitz, & Kennedy, 2003) is offered by way of brief review before moving on to the topic of self-care:

Surviving a life-threatening personal experience often produces intense psychological reactions in the forms of intrusive thoughts about the experience and fear-related avoidance of reminders. In the first few weeks following a traumatic experience these patterns are found in most individuals and thus seem to represent a natural response mechanism for psychological adaptation to a life-changing event. Persistence of this reaction pattern at troublesome levels beyond a three month period, however, indicates that the natural psychological adjustment process, like mourning in the bereaved, has been derailed. At that point the psychological reactions natural in the first few weeks become symptoms of PTSD. In other words, PTSD may be seen as the persistence of a natural process beyond its natural time frame for resolutions.

The cardinal features of PTSD are trauma-specific symptoms of intrusion, avoidance, and physical arousal. The primary requirement is the presence of . . . a life-threatening event, such as serious injury in a traffic accident, [which] would satisfy this criterion, while the expected death of a loved one from natural causes would not. The current diagnostic system then groups PTSD symptoms into three additional categories. [It] includes the presence in some form of persistent intrusive thoughts and feelings. Recurrent distressing dreams or flashbacks while awake about the traumatic experience are examples. . . . [The second category] represents the presence of avoidance symptoms associated with the trauma, such as avoiding driving following a severe traffic accident or fear of sexual relations following sexual assault. More subtle forms of avoidance would be general numbing of responsiveness or the absence of strong feelings about the trauma. . . . [The final category] reflects the presence of symptoms of increased physical arousal and hypervigilance. Feelings of panic may be experienced in situations similar to the trauma; for example, combat veterans with PTSD may show powerful startle reactions to loud noises that resemble gunshots or explosions. . . .

Common elements of traumatic experience include being physically and psychologically overwhelmed by a life-threatening event which is beyond the victim's prediction and control. . . .

Contributions from behavioral psychology help in understanding how PTSD symptoms develop. Pavlovian conditioning occurs at the time of the trauma so that the overpowering feelings of life-threat and helplessness are paired with other cues present (which are not life-threatening). By this learning process these cues acquire the potential for evoking extreme fear when they are encountered later. The survivor also learns that escaping from these cues terminates the distressing fear. Planning life activities to avoid painful reminders, an example of instrumental learning, may become a preferred coping strategy since it reduces the painful exposure to trauma reminders.

From a cognitive psychology perspective, the meaning which the survivor attaches to the traumatic experience may play an important role in PTSD. Perceptions of helplessness associated with the traumatic experience may serve to immobilize survivors' more active coping efforts, thereby serving to maintain PTSD symptoms.

While these approaches are helpful in explaining possible mechanisms for the development of PTSD, they do not explain why some individuals exposed to intense trauma do not develop enduring PTSD symptoms. In order to address this issue an integrative approach is necessary which includes additional factors beyond biological reactivity, Pavlovian and instrumental learning, and symbolic meaning. In our integrative model of PTSD the experience of an overwhelming biological reaction during a life-threatening traumatic event lays the necessary foundation for the development of PTSD through behavioral and cognitive mechanisms of learning. However, other factors serve to mediate between exposure to trauma and the development of PTSD symptoms. Thus, an integrative approach to understanding PTSD includes the interaction between traumatic experiences and other non-trauma factors to account for the development or non-development of PTSD. (Foy, Drescher, Fits, & Kennedy, 2003, pp. 274–277)

Once again, knowing as much as you can about PTSD is essential not only for client/patient care and referral but also for your own health and the welfare of your colleagues and those whom you supervise. When vicarious PTSD disrupts the clinician's frame of reference, the results may change his/her world view, sense of professional and personal identity, and spiritual, psychological, or philosophical outlook. The negative ripple effect may lead to personal alienation from friends, long-term coworkers, and even the relationship one has with oneself. It can cause abrupt and inappropriate job change and a dramatic alteration of one's personality style with and approach to others (e.g., inability to modulate emotions). Extremes such as absenteeism or overinvolvement may not only cause personal problems but also be bad role models for other members of the treatment team. Consequently, as in the case of chronic secondary stress, awareness of this potential problem is essential. And, building on this awareness of the challenges of stress, knowing how to develop a self-care protocol, appreciating the value of solitude, silence, and mindfulness in one's life, and being able to increase one's ongoing level of self-understanding (even in, especially in, difficult situations that may involve failure and loss of life), along with broadening the clinician's own self-view—given the contributions of positive psychology—are essential as well. Accordingly, it is to these topics that we turn next and will devote the majority of this book.

QUESTIONNAIRE 1.1

Clinicians' Vulnerability Profile Questionnaire

- How do you deal with demanding patients?
- How do you blunt ("medicate") the pain you experience in your clinical practice?
- In what instances do you "dump" on coworkers or subordinates?
- What type of person "gets to you"?
- How do you handle the unrealistic expectations of your clients and coworkers?
- What past failures haunt you, and how have you learned from them?
- What prevents you from fully responding to life as a person and social worker, counselor, or psychotherapist?
- How do you handle unscheduled events in the day?
- What are the things that you tend to lie to yourself about or hide from coworkers, patients, and family?
- What triggers your anger most easily?
- What do you feel you are most insecure about?
- What is having the greatest negative impact on both your professional and personal lives?
- How have you addressed the imbalances in your home life (with spouse, children, friends . . .) given the intensity of clinical practice?
- What are the ways you address problems in your department such as under/poor staffing, incompetence/poor work ethic, chronic complaining, rigidity, narrow compartmentalizing of responsibilities and not stepping

beyond these roles, overcompensating by some to deal with weaknesses of others?

- When do you find yourself not listening to family or friends because you feel emotionally exhausted or that their problems aren't as important as those of your patients?
- What themes run through your daydreams and night dreams?
- What recent cases produce in you the most guilt, resentment, or embarrassment?
- When are you the most bored with work, and what do you do about it?
- What are the coping mechanisms you use when you feel overwhelmed?

QUESTIONNAIRE 1.2

Questions to Ask to Uncover Vicarious PTSD in Clinicians

If one or more of the following symptoms/signs have lasted longer than one month and are presently interfering in your personal and professional life, care must be taken to consider that the result of being constantly exposed to persons who have experienced trauma may be having a vicarious impact on clinicians:

1. Do you find that you are reexperiencing past traumatic events?

    a. Nightmares
    b. Intrusive thoughts about patients
    c. Flashbacks to stories patients have shared
    d. Reliving interactions with clients
    e. Association of events in present with past trauma or the traumatic experiences of others

2. Are you experiencing a blunting of affect, numbing, loss of feelings, or tendency to avoid reminders of a past traumatic event?

    a. Feeling a sense of detachment or restriction of range of emotions
    b. Avoiding thoughts, feelings, conversations, people, or activities that are reminders of past traumatic material related by patients

    c. Having memory lacunae with respect to past trauma-laden events

    d. Having a morbid view of the future (e.g., expected shortened length or outlook of remainder of health care career, life span, family life, etc.)

3. Do you have a heightened/exaggerated sense of arousal?

    a. Hyperalert or usually feeling "on guard" in ways similar to sexually/physically abused clients

    b. Pronounced startle reaction

    c. Irritability or a "short emotional fuse" with clients, colleagues, supervisors, and family

    d. Problems concentrating, sleeping, eating, or enjoying normal activities that previously brought you pleasure or provided a sense of mastery

4. Do you experience dramatic alterations in your outlook or world view?

    a. Personal sense of safety/trust is as fragile as clients suffering from PTSD

    b. Positive view of the human condition is absent or overshadowed by a jaded sense of life

    c. View of one's own efficacy as a therapist and personal self-confidence is now questioned

    d. Awareness of cruelty or fragility of life (given the experiences of colleagues or patients whom you have treated) is often present in a depressing, somewhat frightening way

e. Feelings of shame, guilt, depression, or worthlessness are present more and more

5. Have you begun to demonstrate symptoms/exaggerated signs of anti/asocial behavior not present prior to the overwhelming/ongoing exposure to your patients' trauma?

   a. Dangerous behavior (e.g., sexual promiscuity, erratic/aggressive/careless driving patterns, fiscal irresponsibility, poor treatment plan development, violating client/colleague boundaries, etc.)
   b. Extreme irresponsibility in one's personal and professional lives
   c. Alcohol abuse, illegal drug use, self-medication, criminal behavior

6. Are your basic interpersonal relations becoming dramatically affected?

   a. Suspicious, cynical, or hypercritical style is now present
   b. Boundary violations with patients, colleagues, and friends
   c. Loss of interest in activities at home/work
   d. Poor patterns of self-care resulting in alterations in interactions with others
   e. Lack of availability to clients, family, and friends.

CHAPTER TWO

Enhancing Resiliency

*Strengthening One's Own
Self-Care Protocol*

[Therapists] must establish mechanisms to maintain
their own physical and mental health and ways to
get relief from the intensity of the work. . . . one such
mechanism is to have professional outlets, such as
supervision and consultation, to provide information,
perspective, and support. Another is to have personal
outlets for sustenance and recreation away from the
work setting.

—Christine A. Courtois, *Recollections
of Sexual Abuse*

Therapists who work with traumatized people
require an ongoing support system to deal with these
intense reactions. Just as no survivor can recover
alone, no therapist can work with trauma alone.

—Judith Herman, *Trauma and Recovery*

Like many academics, I spent my young adult years
postponing many of the small things that I knew

would make me happy, including reading novels for pleasure, learning to cook, taking a photography class, and joining a gym. I would do all of these things when I had time—when I finished school, when I had a job, when I was awarded tenure, and so on. I was fortunate enough to realize that I would never have time unless I made the time. And then the rest of my life began.

—Christopher Peterson, *A Primer in Positive Psychology*

Care must be taken not to be driven in one's career to the extent that everything else loses value and accordingly does not receive the attention it should. Although being a clinician is a wonderful way to devote oneself to the welfare of others, unless care is taken to ensure that the rest of one's life is fulfilling and balanced as well, one's life becomes too narrow, limited, and eventually distorted. This can have negative impact not only on oneself but also on family life and other interpersonal relations, including one's clients.

In addition to workaholism and narrowing one's horizon so that outside interests, family, and even oneself are left out, as was previously noted, there is the added problem of denial. Most clinicians would probably deal with the dangers of burnout or vicarious PTSD if they were already aware of them. They would also view the elements of stress management in a more respectful, serious manner. Stress management includes basic elements (see appendix E). While clinicians are aware of them with respect to others, sometimes they don't really recognize them as clearly in terms of themselves.

When this is so, people who engage in intense helping roles pay for this in terms of impaired psychological and physical health—not to mention the havoc it wreaks in one's family and on one's necessary social outlets. If clinicians don't pay for it immediately, then—like the clients they work with—eventually they do. The problem with "eventually" is that as with many psychophysical disorders in which psychological stress produces physical changes over time, the damage done, which seems so quiet and may be initially reversible, after a period of time might eventually cause more or less limited irreversible damage (e.g., shingles after age 50). At that point, even when stress is reduced and self-care enriched, the physical harm already done can have chronic implications for the rest of one's life.

Another reality that all of us must deal with is that

the self is limited. It has only so much energy. If it is not renewed, then depletion will take place. Too often we don't avail ourselves of the type of activities that truly renew us. When this occurs we run a greater risk that we will unnecessarily lose perspective and burn out, which is not only sad for us but for the people we are in a position to help in our circle of family, friends, and coworkers. (Wicks, 2003, p. 46)

Sometimes, though, it takes a rude awakening for us to realize how far we have drifted from a balanced life. I certainly can vouch for this personally:

A number of years ago a very close friend of mine in his early forties was dying, from brain cancer. He was outrageous and we constantly teased one another. Even though he was dying, this did not stop.

He had been living in New York and I hadn't seen much of him in the years since I was the best man at his wedding. When he was hospitalized in Philadelphia to undergo experimental treatment, I visited him. When I came to visit he had already been there for almost two weeks.

When I inquired about his health he shared a summary of his condition, which included loss of short-term memory. So, I said to him: "You mean you can't remember what happened yesterday?" He said: "No."

Then I smiled and said: "So, you don't remember me coming in and sitting here with you each day for five hours for the past two weeks?" He looked at me, hesitated for a second or two, grinned widely, and said . . . well I can't share exactly what he said . . . but we both had a good laugh over it.

One of the things he did surprise me with, though, was a question that really helped me put my activities in perspective. He asked: "What good things are you doing now?" As I started to launch into an obsessive (naturally well-organized) list of my recent academic and professional accomplishments, he interrupted me by saying: "No, not that stuff. I mean what really good things have you done? When have you gone fishing last? What museums have you visited lately? What good movies have you seen in the past month?" The "good things" he was speaking about the last time I saw him alive were different from the ones I in my arrogant good health thought about. Unfortunately, I have a lot of company in this regard. (Wicks, 1997, pp. 71–72)

Naturally, what makes up a self-care protocol varies from person to person and differs according to the stage of life we are in. As Baker notes:

> There are many different ways to practice self-care. No one model exists in terms of definition, meaning, significance, or application. Differences between individuals relate to personal history, gender, and personality, and within-individual differences relate to developmental stage, or changing needs. Such differences influence the substance and process of self-care. For one person at a particular stage of life, self-care might involve maintaining a very active schedule and hiring a housekeeper. For another person, or for the same person at a different stage, self-care might involve considerable amounts of quiet, uncommitted personal time and tending one's own home. (2003, pp. 18–19)

Since such a list needs to be tailored, it is helpful to have a large pool of possibilities from which to choose. Listing a number of them here is designed to spur thinking around what could comprise a self-care protocol in your own case. However, there needs to be a sense that the time we spend on self-care is part of the self-respect needed to live a life of true joy rather than a compulsive rat race under the guise that my profession demands constant presence if I am to be seen as someone who takes it seriously. And so, knowing which elements you might entertain as part of a self-care protocol and questions to ponder in the overall development of it are both good initial steps in acting upon the need to take responsibility for oneself.

ELEMENTS OF A SELF-CARE PROTOCOL

There are basic elements of a self-care protocol that most everyone needs to renew themselves on an ongoing basis. It really doesn't require too much to take a step back from our work routine to become refreshed and regain perspective. Some of the basic elements might include:

- Quiet walks by yourself
- Time and space for meditation
- Spiritual and recreational reading—including the diaries and biographies of others whom you admire
- Some light exercise
- Opportunities to laugh offered by movies, cheerful friends, etc.
- A hobby such as gardening
- Phone calls to family and friends who inspire and tease you
- Involvement in projects that renew
- Listening to music you enjoy (Wicks, 2003, p. 50)

Other simple steps at self-care and renewal might be:

- Visiting a park or hiking
- Having family or friends over for dinner or evening coffee
- Going to the library or a mega-bookstore to have coffee, a scone, and to peruse the magazines
- Shopping for little things that would be fun to have but not cost a lot
- Taking a bath rather than a quick shower
- Daydreaming

- Forming a "dining club" in which you go out once a month for lunch with a friend or sibling
- E-mailing friends
- Listening to a mystery book on tape
- Reading poetry out loud
- Staying in bed later than usual on a day off
- Having a leisurely discussion with your spouse over morning coffee in bed
- Watching an old movie
- Making love with your spouse
- Buying and reading a magazine you have never read before
- Fixing a small garden with bright, cheery flowers
- Telephoning someone you haven't spoken to in ages
- Buying and playing a new CD by a singer or musician you love
- Taking a short walk (without listening to music) before and after work and/or during lunchtime
- Going to a diner and having a cup of tea and a piece of pie
- Going on a weekend retreat at a local spirituality center or a hotel on large grounds so you can take out time to walk, reflect, eat when you want, read as long as you'd like, or just renew yourself
- Arranging to spend a couple of days by yourself in your own home without family or friends present just to lounge around and be alone without a schedule or the needs or agendas of others
- Getting a cheap copybook and journaling each day as a way of unwinding

Professionals also have the opportunity for continuing education, research and writing, collaboration with colleagues, mentoring—both receiving and offering it, going on a professional or spiritual miniretreat; the list is endless. The important thing is to recognize the need to intentionally and spontaneously put these elements into your schedule so they represent a constant, significant portion of the time you have available each day/week/month/year.

Domar and Dreher in their trade book *Self-Nurture*, which according to their self-stated goal is primarily written for women but which is filled with good suggestions for anyone concerned about their own welfare, refers to the time available as a "time pie." They suggest that once we prepare our list, we then see how much time, in fact, we really allot for what we say we are interested in doing for ourselves. They write:

Now compare your list . . . with your time pie. How much time is indicated on the pie for any of the activities listed? Of course, there may be pastimes on your list that you wouldn't do that frequently, like going to a comedy club. But others, like daydreaming or reading, might ideally be part of a typical day. Do these activities show up on our time pie? Many women who follow this exercise discover that there is *no* time on their pie for any of the . . . items. Others count the time spent on purely joyful activity in minutes rather than hours. This can be a shocking revelation, one that motivates some women to radically transform the way they spend their time. (2000, p. 198)

QUESTIONS TO PONDER IN THE DEVELOPMENT
OF A SELF-CARE PROTOCOL

Time is a very precious commodity for clinicians. How we allot it, what takes precedence, and with whom we spend it all says a great deal about us and the way we live our lives. In the words of the Dalai Lama in his book *The Path to Tranquility*, "It is very wrong for people to feel deeply sad when they lose some money, yet when they waste the precious moments of their lives they do not have the slightest feeling of repentance" (Dalai Lama, 1999, p. 73). Yet, "waste" for clinicians sometimes means the wrong thing. The feeling for many clinicians is that if I take out time for myself, this leisure period is not "time well spent." Instead, this leisure is seen as almost wrong given all the demands of people experiencing emotional stress or, at the very least, must be earned by conducting a stretch of long therapy hours without any rejuvenating break. To counter this, one must first explore the options available to develop a self-care protocol inventory, which is not a nicety of life but a necessary source of constant renewal so that care for others can be done in a quality fashion over an often long period of time.

Once one reviews such a list, how it is used is crucial. At this point, the challenge that presents itself is: *How do we formulate a protocol that we are likely to use beneficially and regularly rather than in spurts?* To ensure an ongoing systematic program is in place, first the clinician must direct a number of questions to her/himself. This is to avoid the dangers of, on the one hand, being unrealistic in developing a protocol and, on the other, of not being creative and expansive enough. Such questions can also help set the stage for designing a personal self-care protocol (as outlined in questionnaire 2.1 at the end of the chapter). Included among these questions are:

- Given the changes in the social work and mental health systems that have resulted in more client/patient hours, lower status, greater chance for litigation, generally lower financial reward given the importance of the work, and overall insecurity at many levels, what creative ways have you developed to ensure that you don't lose sight of the wonders of being a clinician and the important role you play in being one?
- When someone says "self-care," what image comes to mind? What are the positive and negative aspects of this image? In terms of importance and how realistic it is to develop your own self-care protocol, where do you stand?
- In terms of self-care, what is the difference between professionals in social work and mental health versus other caregivers?
- How do you balance your time alone to renew your energy, reflect on your life, and clear your thinking with the time you spend with those who challenge, support, and make you laugh?
- Self-care and self-knowledge go hand in hand. What types of activities (e.g., structured reflection at the end of a day, informal debriefing of oneself during the drive home, journaling, mentoring, therapy, spiritual guidance, reading, etc.) are you involved in which will help you develop a systematic and ongoing analysis of how you are progressing in life?

- What types of exercise (walking, the gym, swimming, exercise machine, etc.) do you enjoy and feel would be realistic for you to be involved in *on a regular basis*?
- Who in your circle of friends provides you with encouragement, challenge, perspective, laughter, and inspiration? How do you ensure that you have ongoing contact with them?
- The balance between work and leisure, professional time and personal time, varies from person to person. What is the ideal balance for you? What steps have you taken to ensure this balance is kept?
- As was previously noted, there is a Russian proverb that says: "When you live next to the cemetery, you can't cry for everyone who dies." Self-care involves not getting pulled into the dramatic emotions, fears, and anger that pervade health care settings. What are the self-care elements that support a healthy sense of detachment?
- Being too conservative or being a procrastinator at one end of the spectrum versus being impulsive or too quick to act in the mental health or social work setting at the other end are extremes that can be dangerous. How do you maintain a sense of balance that prevents behavior at either extreme of the spectrum?
- How do you prepare for change, which is such a natural part of clinical work?
- What is the best way you can balance between stimulation and time in silence and solitude so you don't have constant stimulation on the one hand or isolation and preoccupation with self on the other?

- How do you process "unfinished business" (e.g., therapeutic failure, duplicity in one's colleagues, past negative events, hurts, fears, lost relationships, etc.) in your life so that you have enough energy to deal with the challenges and appreciate the joys in front of you?
- What do you number among the stable forces in your life that are anchors for your own sense of well-being and self-care?
- In what way do you ensure that your goals are challenging and high but not unrealistic and deflating?
- What self-care steps do you have to take because of your gender or race that others of a different gender or race don't have to take?
- How has your past experience set habits in motion that make self-care a challenge in some ways?
- What self-care steps are more important at this stage of your life than they were at earlier life stages?
- What emotional and physical "red flags" are you aware of which indicate that you must take certain self-care steps so as not to burn out, violate boundaries, medicate yourself in unhealthy ways, withdraw when you shouldn't, verbally attack patients or colleagues, or drown yourself in work?
- What do you *already* do in terms of self-care? In each of the following areas, what have you found to be most beneficial: physical health, interactions with a circle of friends, professionally, financially, psychologically, and spiritually?
- What is the next step you need to take in developing your self-care protocol? How do you plan to bring this about?

- Are your holidays and vacations appropriately spaced and sufficient for your needs? What is the most renewing way for you to spend this time?
- Are you also conscious of the need for "daily holidays" involving a brief tea or coffee break, a short walk, playing with the children in the evening, or visiting one's friends or parents? Practicing a putt in one's office or living room, shopping, casting with a fly rod in a neighborhood field?

Reflecting on these questions periodically and responding honestly to all of them can improve self-knowledge in ways that aid in burnout prevention. They also can increase sensitivity to how you live your life in a way that enables you to both flourish personally and become more faithful and passionate professionally. Once again, the way one moves through the day depends a great deal on personality style. *Burnout is not from the amount of work but how we perceive it and interact with people as we do it.* Some people complain that they are so busy that they don't have time to breathe. Others with the same schedule intensity reflect on how happy they are that they are involved in so many challenging projects. All, on the other hand, would complain about the amount of paperwork and documentation that is necessary in modern mental health and social work.

Some of us love exercise and thrive on it. Others are more sedentary in our existence. All of us, though, want to be physically healthy. Not everyone likes outdoor activities and vacations packed with touring new sites and experiencing adventures in different parts of the country or world. Some of us prefer the back yard, a leisurely walk, an artist's easel, a fishing pole, a good book, or a familiar restaurant. However, all of us like to have time away at different points.

The differences among us are many. That is why each self-care protocol, if it is to be both realistic and effective, is unique in its composition. The important point, though, is that we must have one in place that we use as a guide every day and not use rationalizations and excuses for not doing this. Not to have a personal self-care protocol is not only courting disaster in terms of both one's personal and professional lives; it is also, at its core, an act of profound disrespect for oneself.

When we have true self-respect that is evidenced by a sound self-care protocol, it can be transformative for us—but, as has been alluded to elsewhere in this book, not just for us but for others as well because one of the greatest gifts we can share with our coworkers and patients is a sense of our own peace and self-respect. However, you can't share what you don't have. It is as simple as that.

Also, we need to recognize that when we speak about self-care and self-nurturing, we are not referring here to another intense program that just adds more stress to life in the name of reducing it. Once again, as Domar and Dreher note:

> True body-nurture absolutely includes physical activity and sound nutrition, but not compulsive exercise and onerous dietary restriction. True body-nurture is also much more than exercise and nutrition. It includes the following actions and ideas:
>
> - Deep diaphragmatic breathing
> - A regular practice of relaxation
> - Cognitive restructuring of body-punishing thoughts into thoughts of compassion and forgiveness

- Delight in the sensual and sexual pleasures of the body
- A sane, balanced, non-shame-based relationship with food
- Health-promoting behaviors, such as stopping smoking, alcohol in moderation, and regular visits to the doctor for preventive care
- A profound regard for the sacredness of the body, including all its functions, imperfections, idiosyncrasies, and wonders. (2000, p. 99)

Such an overall approach to body-nurture and the other approaches mentioned thus far will clearly benefit us and help us develop an attitude and behaviors that will improve health and increase personal and professional well-being. Before closing this brief treatment of the topic of self-care, though, I would also like to at least address the topics of "toxic work" and time management and discuss two particular elements of a self-care protocol (reading and friendship) that I feel are especially important in order to provide a model of how you can take each part of a self-care protocol and personally develop it more deeply as a way of seeing how it can support and challenge you. Finally, a basic broad-based questionnaire designed to aid in the development of one's own self-care protocol (questionnaire 2.1) given what has been covered in this chapter is provided at the end of this chapter. It provides a summary of the contents of the chapter and may offer a succinct illustration of what the reader feels self-care involves for him/herself. Completing and reflecting upon it alone, with a mentor, or in a group of colleagues can be revealing and instructive as to what areas might need more or less emphasis in the future.

TOXIC WORK

In her book *Toxic Work*, Barbara Bailey Reinhold notes:

> The syndrome of toxic work overtakes you when what's happening to you at work causes protracted bouts of distress, culminating in emotional suffering or physical symptoms and heightened by the perceived inability to stop the pain and move on to find or create a more rewarding situation. Feeling stuck where you are, unable to imagine or take your next steps, is perhaps the most debilitating part of the problem. (1997, p. 15)

She also points out that this level of psychological "toxicity" is not going to get better in the near future and that we can

> Expect more pressure, greater demands, and fewer people employed on-site to do the work. . . . Cost-cutting will be the official support of most organizations both for-profits and nonprofits; budgets will run very close to the wire. . . . Uncertainty will prevail. The only thing you can count on is your own ability to land on your feet. . . . Constant learning will be required particularly in technology [and] . . . You'll need to take responsibility for choreographing your own career and underwriting your own retirement; formerly paternalistic organizations have gotten out of the business of taking care of people. (pp. 34–35)

This sounds very much like what is going on today in modern mental health and social work, and responding to it with a sense of negativity or being nostalgic for the "good old days," while understandable, will not carry us today. Again, in the words of the author of *Toxic Work*, who offers an example from nursing that can well apply to persons serving as clinicians:

> Marjorie, a nurse in the day-surgery unit, told me, "We can't wait for this time of cost-cutting to be over, so we can go back to practicing the way we were trained." . . . She belonged to a cadre of "good old days" complainers who gathered in the hospital snack bar at break time each morning. . . .
>
> Fortunately, Marjorie had a friend in pediatrics who had stopped going to the "bitch and moan" sessions, as she called them, because she believed they made things worse. . . . "These are the new policies, and they're not going away," she told Marjorie, "so why don't we go to the hospital fitness room together tomorrow and ride the stationary bikes instead?" Marjorie tried it, was shocked at how different it made her feel. (Reinhold, 1997, p. 105)

What Reinhold is pointing out is that if you or other colleagues are having a difficult time letting go of percepts of what was in the past, then this is, in her description, a toxic situation that requires healthy actions.

Such healthy actions include the elements of a self-care protocol thus far included in this chapter, an awareness of the dangers of chronic and acute secondary stress noted in chapter 1, a willingness to draw from the mindfulness literature so we can strengthen our inner lives (to be addressed in chapter 3), and a balanced sense of ourselves (given the recent contributions of positive psychology), so we can be healthy and flexible enough to deal with a constantly changing environment (to be covered in chapter 4). In addition, we will find in all books addressing the toxic work environment and the topic of self-care a need to be aware of how we organize and manage our time.

TIME MANAGEMENT

An essential part of self-care is being respectful of the limited time that we have available during the day. Each clinician needs to have some level of awareness of this issue so that energy is not unduly wasted. For instance, emergency medical services personnel (EMS) are advised as follows:

1. *Schedule personal time in each day*: Alone time allocated for exercise, meditation, a hobby, or some activity is crucial to the quality of your personal and professional life.
2. *Delegate*: When appropriate at work or home, learn to delegate responsibilities. When you delegate, explain instructions clearly, assign a completion time or date with each task, and follow up once the task is completed. Give positive feedback when appropriate.
3. *Schedule interruptions*: Learn to be flexible in your schedule and off-the-job plans if the phone rings while you're at home.
4. *Organize*: You can save precious time if you have a designated place for [materials you frequently use in your practice.]

5. *Access your resources*: Learn what resources are available to help you do what needs to be done. Learn where these resources are and when you can use them.

6. *Learn to recognize your physical and mental limitations*: Learn *how* and *when* to say no (e.g., "I'm sorry, but I simply don't have time"). Be gentle but firm.

7. Time management is not a control of time. Rather, it is your ability to use your time more efficiently when personal responsibilities accumulate. Time management techniques themselves can be stressful if careful planning and flexibility aren't built into the process. (Seaward, 2000, p. 45)

In his eminently practical book *The Successful Physician*, Marshall Zaslove also includes a discussion of a number of ways medical professionals can improve their productivity. I believe that much of what he has to say is also quite relevant and practical for mental health and social work professionals to consider as well. His belief is that just working harder and longer is not the solution. Some of his ideas and recommendations I believe would be beneficial for a clinician to reflect upon and discuss with one's colleagues or mentor are:

- We are not as efficient as we think we are and must start managing ourselves and our careers if we are to be more effective.
- Professional goals provide a psychological rudder, offer us something to focus on and look forward to,

help us set priorities, and measure our progress in what our achievements are.

- Looking at areas where time is wasted and doing what you can to prune what is unnecessary will lead to a schedule that is professionally richer and more personally satisfying.
- One of the most costly time wasters is interruptions—seek to limit them with assertiveness and clear feedback to those around you.
- Find your own natural rhythm and work with it.
- Be as attentive as you can when focusing on patients and their problems.
- Design your own ongoing professional education to meet your personal needs.
- Use methods that save time (skim articles . . .) and integrate knowledge as it relates to actual cases so learning is tailored to the type of cases you are handling rather than simply general or theoretical in nature.
- Have your own panel of experts and knowledge network so you can better learn from your own and others' errors. (Zaslove, 2001, pp. 166–168)

With just a little attention to personal organization and productivity, so much stress could be reduced. However, frequently little is done in this area. The feeling may be that this is the kind of information important for people in business or that it is beneath the level of social work and mental health professionals. Obviously, though, when we think of how this would improve client care, collegiality, and enrich the personal life of the clinician, such views are out of touch with their multifaceted demanding life.

Similarly, not to develop each aspect of a self-care protocol is also foolish and dangerous because as was emphasized earlier, one of the greatest gifts we can share with our patients is a sense of our own peace, confidence, and energy. And so, each element in such a protocol is worth delving into and developing as completely as possible. To illustrate what I mean by this, I offer the examples below of how both *reading* and *friendship*—when examined as completely as possible—can truly support and challenge us and offer us a new sense of perspective with respect to both our personal and professional life.

Reading

Once, peace activist Dorothy Day was sitting conversing with a homeless alcoholic woman. She confessed to Ms. Day that one of the steps she had to take to remain sober was to close her eyes when passing a bar. In response, Dorothy Day said with a commiserating smile, "I know what you mean. I have to do the same thing when I pass a bookstore" (Day, source unknown).

With the publication of the Harry Potter novels, many children who did not read longer length books began joyfully jumping into them. Mega-bookstores with cafes that are open late now attract people and tempt them by magazines and books to read more. Yet, many of us still don't read enough. One excuse is a seeming lack of time or energy to do so. However, reading—professional or otherwise—can provide new perspectives that may even instill new energy, helpful contexts, and, in the end, save wasted preoccupation or avoid unnecessary drains on our resources.

Professional continuing education, research, and reading aren't just another chore but a lifeline to perspective and passion. But reading and the nourishment it offers us go well beyond professional material, as important as that is. We must take steps to improve our overall style of reading as part of a comprehensive approach to self-care; the following is a reflection that relates directly to this topic:

Years ago when I was an undergraduate student, the chairperson of the philosophy department and I discussed various interests. Once, when the topic of reading fiction came up, he said that he set aside twenty minutes each night for reading a novel. To this statement I made a facial expression which gave him the message: "Is that all the fiction you read?" In response to my look, he said: "Twenty minutes each night on a regular basis is a heck of a lot of fiction over the period of a year, Bob." And, of course, he was right.

The important first element in having a reading plan for ourselves so that our hearts are nourished by the ideas, themes, challenges, and hopes of others is for us to set up *regular times to read* to which we will be faithful. Once this is done, we can then address two other issues in developing a reading plan. They are *breadth* and *depth.*

Breadth and Depth

Even persons who read a great deal still run the risk of getting caught in a rut. Some of us may only read certain types of novels, a particular type of devotional material, or solely material of a certain genre. Just as in the case of our physical well-being, our spiritual health depends upon a varied and balanced "diet" of good reading. Such a diet should include: good fiction, autobiographies/biographies, journals, general non-fiction, books of quotations, poetry . . . books of contemporary and "classic" spirituality. . . .

Good Fiction

In addition to the type of novels we normally enjoy, reading other types of books which challenge and open us up is a good idea. The best-seller list is not the only source of ideas for such reading—as a matter of fact, today it may even be misleading! Winners of the Booker Prize, the Pulitzer, and the National Book Award, as well as suggestions from good friends, might be better sources. The question "What good books have you read recently?" is a good one to ask of friends whose taste and commitment to a life of meaning you respect.

Autobiographies/Biographies

In the introduction to The Radcliffe Biography Series, Matina S. Horner writes: "Fine biographies give us both a glimpse of ourselves and a reflection of the human spirit. Biography illuminates history, inspires by example, and fires the imagination to life's possibilities. Good biography can create lifelong models for us. Reading about other people's experiences encourages us to persist, to face hardship, and to feel less alone. Biography tells us about choice, the power of a personal vision, and the interdependence of human life."

Reading contemporary autobiographies such as Maya Angelou's *I Know Why the Caged Bird Sings* (Bantam, 1971), Etty Hillesum's *An Interrupted Life* (Pocket Books, 1985), the Dalai Lama's *Freedom in Exile* (Harper, 1991) or Thomas

Merton's *Seven Storey Mountain* (Harcourt, Brace and Jovanovich, 1948) all bear out Dr. Horner's comments. Also, reading biographies such as Robert Cole's *Dorothy Day: A Radical Devotion* (Addison-Wesley, 1987) or A. N. Wilson's biography of C. S. Lewis (Norton, 1990) brings us into the world of persons who can help us see life differently than we might, given our own limited background. The possibilities of both autobiographies and biographies, contemporary and classic, are often overlooked by many of us for more "attractive, exciting reading." Once exposed to this type of book, though, we begin to see that real adventure is entering deeply into the life of another—especially one who faced the despair of life and didn't give in to the situation.

Journals

Journals are another way to follow the movements and nuances of people's lives. They, like biographies, also can be quite nourishing and challenging to our souls. Dag Hammarskjold's *Markings* (Knopf, 1976), Kathleen Norris' *Dakota* (Houghton-Mifflin, 1992), Henri Nouwen's *The Genesee Diary* (Doubleday, 1981), and Thomas Merton's *A Vow of Conversation* (Farrar, Straus, and Giroux, 1993) put us in a place where we can explore, piece by piece, the thinking and reactions of individuals trying to make spiritual sense out of the daily occurrences of their lives.

Diaries help us to travel through a geography of reflection which can serve only to help deepen our own sense of healthy introspection. In addition, as we view the diaries of others, their quality of self-understanding can help us move away from morbid and mundane preoccupation with self. They can inspire us to reach out to the world instead of being drawn into a secure quietistic shell of moody self-involvement.

Books of Quotes/Short Reflections

Years ago in New York City, there were several wonderful authentic Swedish smorgasbords. I just loved them. Such variety! Such quality samplings! Now they are gone, and the brutal buffets of so-so samplings have replaced them throughout the city. As a matter of fact, unfortunately, such blah buffets are everywhere.

A similar scene can be observed with books of quotes. They have proliferated as people seek more and more easy ways to nourish themselves emotionally and spiritually. As a result, motivations regarding why one is seeking such a collection is an important factor in gathering up a volume of quotes for reflection.

If the goal is to sustain oneself on such volumes, then no matter how good a choice made, one's spiritual life will be kept fairly superficial by the use of them. Yet, if books of this type are used as a way to sample wide varieties of hearts and minds and to supplement a regular reading regimen, the results can be quite wonderfully beneficial.

Selection of the type of collection is obviously as important as the place enjoying such material plays in one's reading habits. There are many superb collections of quotes/short reflections available for our use. Anthony de Mello's *One Minute Wisdom* (Doubleday, 1986), Carolyn Warner's *The Last Word* (Prentice-Hall, 1992), and *The Great Thoughts* compiled by George Seldes (Bantam, 1985) are only three that quickly come to mind, but of course there are many more. So, spending a few minutes in a bookstore skimming through selections that initially seem of interest is always a good idea before deciding on which one to buy.

Poetry Books

Most of us read only a line or two of poetry every now and then in a magazine. However, the poetry of such persons as Rilke, Yeats, Frost, or e.e. cummings can break through our fixed ways of viewing life.

Poets see life in such a pristine way that we can be borne up by them to a vantage point we might never see if it weren't for their use of language and meter. . . .

Spirituality Books

Volumes specifically designed to help us gain a deeper understanding of our connection to what and Who is greater than our own lives are obviously important as well . . . moving beyond one's own tradition to read from other religious traditions is also very enlightening and inspiring. (Wicks, 1998, pp. 63–67)

And so, reading can bring psychological and spiritual nourishment in so many ways *if* we avail ourselves of it in a structured way that involves time, breadth, and depth in our selections. As Kottler also recognizes specifically with respect to the reading habits of clinicians:

Freud found the fiction of Dostoyevsky, Sophocles, and Shakespeare . . . the philosophy of Mill and Nietzsche to be the inspiration for his theories. It was not his formal medical training as much as his readings of *King Lear, Hamlet, Oedipus Rex,* and *The Brothers Karamazov* that formed the cornerstone of theories. Freud was first and foremost an integrationist who was able to draw on the wisdom of poets, sculptors, neurologists, philosophers, playwrights, and his patients to create a unified vision of the human world. (1989, p. 35)

A final suggestion in this area is to include time for reflection on what you have read. I actually underline in the books I read and copy out some of those underlined passages if I feel they are truly important to keeping perspective and hope alive within me. Finally, I review the comments several times during the week or month so I can make the lessons they hold a part of the way I live. I have also found that the impact of this on those I mentor to be quite impressive because the lessons are so available to me when I need them.

Friendship and Community

As well as reading, one of the other key aspects of self-care is to have a well-rounded circle of friends. Anthropologist Margaret Meade once noted that "one of the oldest human needs is having someone to wonder where you are when you don't come home at night" (Meade, source unknown). Psychology has long emphasized the need to relate as a key element of health and happiness. As Baker notes in her book on self-care for psychologists:

To care for our self in relationship with others, we must actively nurture our relationships with our significant other, children, family of origin, friends, and colleagues. Connecting with others beyond our immediate circle of relationships can be equally important; participation in community organizations can help us feel connected to a larger whole. . . . The quality of our relationships, more than the quantity, is key. In both our personal and professional lives our best relationships are those in which we can be as close to our true self as possible. (2003, p. 127)

For all major spiritual traditions, "community" is also an essential element. Yet, as Baker has just noted, *who* is in that community is just as significant as the recognition that we should be part of one. As psychologist and spiritual writer Henri Nouwen recognizes:

We can take a lot of physical and even mental pain when we know that it truly makes us a part of the life we live together in the world. But when we feel cut off from the human family, we quickly lose heart. (1981, p. 33)

An absence of at least one significant friend may have physical consequences as well:

Redford Williams, M.D., of Duke University, tracked almost 1,400 men and women who underwent coronary angiograms and were found to have at least one severely blocked coronary artery. After five years, those who were unmarried and who did not have at least one close confidante were over three times more likely to have died than people who were married, had one or more confidantes, or both. (Domar and Dreher, 2000, p. 213)

In my work and that which I have done with others (Wicks and Hamma, 1996; Wicks, 1992), I have found that for the circle to be rich, we need, at the very least, four "types" or "voices" present (since one friend may play different beneficial roles at different points in our lives). They are: the *prophet*, the *cheerleader*, the *harasser*, and the *guide*. By having these "voices" in our lives, the chances are greater that we will be able to maintain a sense of perspective, openness, and balance. A brief description of each follows.

The Prophet

The first of these voices which helps us maintain balance and have a sense of openness is the one I shall refer to as the prophet. Contrary to what one might imagine, prophetic friends need not look or behave any differently than other types of persons who are close to us. . . . The true prophet's voice is often quiet and fleeting, but nonetheless strong. She or he is living an honest courageous life guided by truth and compassion. . . . They are trying to live out the truth, and whether knowingly or not, they follow the advice of Gandhi: "Let our first act every morning be this resolve: I shall not fear anyone on earth. I shall fear only God. I shall not bear ill-will toward anyone. I shall conquer untruth by truth and in resisting untruth, I shall put up with all suffering."

The message of prophets often involves discomfort or pain, not masochistic pain but real pain. Often they do not directly produce conflict. Instead, like leaders in the nonviolent movement, they "merely" set the stage for it, as is pointed out in the following words of Martin Luther King, Jr.:

> We who engage in nonviolent, direct action are not the creators of tension. We merely bring to the surface the hidden tension that is already alive. We bring it out in the open, where it can be seen and dealt with. Like a boil that can never be cured so long as it is covered up but must be opened with all its ugliness to the natural medicines of air and light, injustice must be exposed, with all the tension its exposure creates, to the light of human conscience and the air of national opinion before it can be cured.

Having someone prophetic in our lives is never easy. No matter how positive we may believe the ultimate consequences will be for us, many of us still shy away from prophetic messages and would readily agree with Henry Thoreau: "If you see someone coming to do you a good deed, run for your life!" However, to seek comfort in lieu of the truth may mean that in an effort to avoid pain, we will also avoid responding to opportunities of real value, real life. We will merely exist and eventually die without having ever really lived. . . . Prophets point! They point to the fact that it doesn't matter whether pleasure or pain is involved, the only thing that matters is . . . that we seek to see and live "the truth" because only it will set us free.

In doing this, prophets challenge us to look at how we are living our lives, to ask ourselves: "To what voices am I listening when I form my attitudes and take my actions each day?"

The Cheerleader

Ironically, one of the most controversial suggestions I might make with respect to friendship is to suggest we all need "cheer-leaders." . . . Some might say that to encourage this type of friend is to run the risk of narcissism and denial. However, to balance the prophetic voices . . . we also need unabashed, enthusiastic, unconditional acceptance by certain people in our lives. Prophecy can and should instill appropriate guilt to break through the crusts of our denial. But guilt cannot sustain us for long. While guilt will push us to do good things because they are right, love encourages us to do the right thing because it is natural.

We can't go it alone. We need a balance of support. We need encouragement and acceptance as much as we need the criticism and feedback that are difficult to hear. Burnout is always around the corner when we don't have people who are ready to encourage us, see our gifts clearly, and be there for us when our involvement with people, their sometimes unrealistic demands, and our own crazy expectations for ourselves, threaten to pull us down. . . . So, while having buoyantly supportive friends may seem like a luxury, make no mistake about it—it is a necessity that is not to be taken lightly. The "interpersonal roads" of time are strewn with well-meaning helpers who tried to survive without such support. Encouragement is a gift that should be treasured in today's stressful, anxious, complex world because the seeds of involvement and the seeds of burnout are the same. To be involved is to risk. And to risk without the presence of solidly supportive friends is foolhardy and dangerous.

The Harasser

When singer-activist Joan Baez was asked her opinion about [contemplative, monk and writer] Thomas Merton, one of the things she said was that he was different than many of the phoney gurus she had encountered in her travels. She said that although Merton took important things seriously in his life, he didn't take himself too seriously. She indicated that he knew how to laugh at situations and particularly at himself. . . . "Harassers" help us to laugh at ourselves and to avoid the emotional burnout resulting from having the unrealistic expectation that people will always follow our guidance or appreciate what we do for them. This type of friend helps us regain and maintain perspective (so we don't unnecessarily waste valuable energy). This is truly a gift for which we can be thankful.

The Guide

The three types of friends we've looked at thus far are each part of a necessary community. The prophet enhances our sense of single-heartedness. The cheerleader generously showers us with the support we feel we need. The harasser encourages us to maintain a sense of proper perspective. Complementing these three is a cluster that, for lack of a better name, shall be referred to as "spiritual guides." . . . guides listen to us carefully and don't accept the "manifest content" (what we say and do) as being equal to the "total content" (our actual intentions plus our statements and actions). Instead, they search and look for nuances in what we share with them to help us to uncover some of the "voices" that are unconsciously guiding our lives, especially the ones that . . . make us hesitant, anxious, fearful, and willful. (Wicks, 1992, pp. 96–111)

To determine whether or how these voices are present in our lives, several questions or statements seeking further information about the composition of our circle of friends might be helpful:

- Do I have people with whom I can simply be myself?
- What type of friends do I value most? Why?
- What do I feel are the main qualities of friendship?
- List and briefly describe the friends who are now in my life.
- Describe ones who are no longer alive or present to me now but who have made an impact on my life. Why do I think they made such a difference in my life?
- Among my circle of friends, who are my personal heroes or role models?
- Who are the prophets in my life? In other words, who confronts me with the question: To what voices am I responding in life?
- Who helps me see my relationships, mission in life, and self-image more clearly? How do they accomplish this?
- Who encourages me in a genuine way through praise and a nurturing spirit?
- Who teases me into gaining a new perspective when I am too preoccupied or tied up in myself?
- When and with whom do I play different (prophetic, supportive . . .) roles as a friend? How do people receive such interactions? (Wicks, 1997, pp. 69–70)

Having a healthy and balanced circle of friends can aid in stress prevention and personal-professional growth. This is an obvious reality. The important point here is that with some attention to this area, we can immeasurably improve the role that encouraging, challenging, and guiding friendships can have in our lives.

By taking each element of a self-care protocol and developing it as was done above with respect to reading and friendship, one can create a rich tapestry of activities and approaches to self-understanding and renewal. First, though, it is important to create a broad enough outline that would comprise the elements of a personally designed self-care protocol given your own needs, work, family life, personality style, and stage of life. To this end, this chapter is concluded by providing a suggested format (questionnaire 2.1) to use as a springboard in the development of what might support, challenge, and give you perspective as you continue to work in one of the most demanding and rewarding professions one can possibly have: *being a clinician.*

QUESTIONNAIRE 2.1

Self-Care Protocol Questionnaire for Clinicians

Please note: This material is for your own use. There is a tendency on some people's part to be quick, terse, and often global in their responses. Such approaches, while natural, limit the helpfulness of completing this questionnaire to gain as full an awareness as possible of your current profile and the personal goals you plan to develop for a realistic yet appropriately balanced and rich self-care program. Consequently, in preparing this personally designed protocol, the more clear, specific, complete, imaginative, and realistic your responses are to the questions provided, the more useful the material will be in integrating it within your schedule.

1. List healthy *nutritional practices* that you currently have in place.
2. What are specific realistic ways to improve your eating/drinking (of alcoholic beverages) habits?
3. What *physical exercise* do you presently get, and when is it scheduled during the week?
4. What changes in your schedule in terms of time, frequency, and variety with respect to exercise do you wish to make?
5. Where are the periods for reflection, quiet time, meditation, minibreaks alone, opportunities to center yourself, and personal debriefing times now in your schedule?
6. Given your personality style, family life, and work situation, what changes would you like to make in your schedule to make it more intentional and balanced with respect to processing what comes to the fore in your time spent alone or in silence?

7. How much, what type, and how deeply and broadly do you read at this point?

8. What would you like to do to increase variety or depth in your reading, research, and continuing education pursuits?

9. Below, list activities present in your nonworking schedule not previously noted above. Alongside the frequency/time, list changes to this schedule that you feel would further enrich you personally/professionally as well as have a positive impact, in turn, on your family, colleagues, and overall social network.

Leisure time with:
    Spouse/Significant other
    Children
    Parents
    Family members
    Friends
Going to movies
Watching TV
Visiting museums
Sports
Attending concerts/plays
Listening to music
Hiking, biking, walking, or swimming
Phone calls to family and friends
Hobbies (gardening, coin collecting, etc.)
Dinner out
Shopping

Visiting libraries, bookstores, coffee shops
E-mailing friends
Making love
Journaling
Continuing education
Vacations
Long weekends away
Meditation/reflection/sitting zazen
Religious rituals
Leisurely baths
Massage
Other activities not listed above:

10. What are the ways you process strong emotions (e.g., anger, anxiety, deep sadness, confusion, fear, emotional "highs," or the desire to violate boundaries for reasons of personal/sexual/financial/power gratification)?
11. Where in your schedule do you regularly undertake such emotional processing?
12. What would you like to do to change the extent of and approaches you are now using for self-analysis/debriefing of self?
13. Who comprises the interpersonal anchors in your life?
14. What do you feel is lacking in your network of friends?
15. What are some reasonable initiatives you wish to undertake to have a richer network?
16. What are your sleep/rest habits now?

17. If you are not getting enough sleep/rest, what are some realistic ways to ensure you get more?

Note: This is just a partial questionnaire. Please feel free to include, analyze, and develop a plan for improvement and integration of other aspects of self-care. Also, review your answers at different points to see what resistances to change come up and how you can face them in new, creative ways by yourself or with the help of a friend, colleague, mentor, or professional counselor or therapist.

CHAPTER THREE

Replenishing the Self

Solitude, Silence, and Mindfulness

I think that any man who watches three football
games in a row should be declared legally dead.

—Erma Bombeck, humorist

What if you missed your life like a person misses
a train?

—Walker Percy, physician and novelist

Mindfulness is living with your eyes wide open.

—Marsha Linehan, *This One Moment*

In his biography of the author Ernest Hemingway, K. S. Lynn offers
the following observation:

The substance of a famous speech in James's *The Ambassadors*
likewise left a deep impression on Hemingway, as one of the
key speeches in *The Sun Also Rises* reveals. "Listen Jake," Robert
Cohn says in the second chapter. "Don't you ever get the feeling that all your life is going by and you're not taking advantage

of it? Do you realize you've lived nearly half the time you have to live already?" In more casual parlance, Cohn is echoing the words of James's Lambert Strether, as he unburdens himself to Little Bilham in Gloriani's beautiful Parish garden. "Live all you can; it's a mistake not to. It doesn't so much matter what you do in particular, so long as you have your life. If you haven't had that, what *have* you had?" (1987, pp. 328–329)

Having "a life" is more than the absence or minimization of negative occurrences. Whereas the source of all stress cannot—and probably should not—be prevented, the way it impacts a clinician does not have to be totally negative. As a matter of fact, amid the suffering, maybe even *because* of it, when one has a sense of meaning in one's life, then a strong appreciation of both the welcome and unwelcome aspects of life and all they hold becomes possible. Clinicians have an opportunity to become even deeper and more compassionate because of the stress if they are mindful and have a healthy sense of perspective.

For instance, one physician who was working in Somalia during a devastating famine was approached by an interviewer for National Public Radio with the following question: "Doctor, how can you stand all of this carnage? The old people are dropping like flies. And the children are dying in such numbers that you are stacking them up in the corner like firewood rather than burying them immediately. How can you stand it?" (You could hear the pain in his voice.) The physician stopped, turned to the interviewer, and said: "When you watch this horror on television in the U.S., you are overwhelmed, aren't you?" When the reporter from NPR nodded, the physician went on: "Well, we in-country feel the same pain *but* there is one difference." The interviewer in an incredulous voice asked: "*What* difference?" And the physician softly responded: "You can't lose hope as long as you are making friends."

Like physicians and other caregivers, how clinicians *perceive* their work, the events that take place during the day, and the people they encounter along the way makes all the difference. Due to this, an increasing number of clinicians I have encountered now seem to use aspects of the literature on solitude, silence, and mindfulness to maintain a sense of psychological perspective. The feeling now seems to be that it would be as foolish to disregard this information as it would be to ignore new theoretical and clinical advances simply because we are unfamiliar with them.

As Cozolino notes in his book *The Making of a Therapist*:

Unlike with other professions, being a competent therapist requires a simultaneous exploration of one's inner world and private thoughts. When we begin training, we embark on two simultaneous journeys: one outward into the professional world and the other inward, through the labyrinths of our own psyches. . . . Over the years, I have had many students who desired to become therapists while sealing off their inner worlds. They tried to stay "above the neck" in the hope of avoiding their own feelings and emotions. I often felt sadness when interacting with these trainees because I could sense the pain beneath their need for disconnection. Unfortunately, this intellectualizing defense handicaps both personal growth and the development of good therapeutic abilities. For most students of psychotherapy, the primary challenge is not mastering the academic material, it is summoning the emotional courage to move through the inner space that leads to knowing oneself. The more fearless we become in the exploration of our inner worlds, the greater our self-knowledge and our ability to help clients. (2004, pp. xv, xvi)

Visvas is a Sanskrit word. Literally translated, it means "to have trust, to breathe freely, to be without fear." Being able to offer yourself, your colleagues, and your patients encounters marked by such "inner psychological space" can make all the difference in clinical work and personal interactions. It is irrelevant whether we say that the approach is based on our perspective, attitude, outlook, or the more inclusive term "inner life."

The "inner world" or "interior life" is what some point to as a place where nonjudgmental self-awareness, simplicity, freedom, and truth flourish. It is the setting in which deeply felt needs are experienced and addressed. These include:

> A need for permanence in a civilization of transience . . .
> A need for silence in the midst of noise;
> A need for gratuitousness in the face of unbelievable greed;
> A need for poverty amid the flaunting of wealth;
> A need for contemplation [or mindfulness meditation] in a century of action, for without contemplation, action risks becoming mere agitation;
> A need for communication in a universe content with entertainment and sensationalism;
> A need for peace amid today's universal outbursts of violence;
> A need for quality to counterbalance the increasingly prevalent response to quantity;

A need for humility to counteract the arrogance of power and science;

A need for human warmth when everything is being rationalized or computerized;

A need to belong to a small group rather than to be part of the crowd;

A need for slowness to compensate the present eagerness for speed;

A need for truth when the real meaning of words is distorted in political speeches and sometimes even in religious discourses;

A need for transparency when everything seems opaque.

Yes, a need for *the interior life*. (Dubois, 1983, pp. 273–274)

The "interior life" includes those psychological factors or schemata that provide us with inner strength, a sound attitude, and a sense of honesty or transparency. Different psychological methods, nontheistic philosophies (e.g., Buddhism), and world spiritualities emphasize various approaches. However, as we look across the board at them, the three themes that seem to resonate, no matter what the approach, are *solitude*, *silence*, and *mindfulness*. These represent more than techniques and timing for persons who believe that seeking more balance and depth is essential. I learned this personally a number of years ago during one of my regular visits to a mentor.

The sessions I had with him helped me keep perspective. At the time, I was (as I am now) in the process of helping other health professionals face their own challenges, darkness, stress, and changes. As one might expect, in helping them face their own secondary stress, anxiety, despair, and darkness, it was psychologically dangerous for me as well. My mentor knew this and called me not to retreat but to go deeper in my own life. The following reflection on the interaction between the two of us, I believe, illustrates this clearly:

> Several months ago [we were walking] through the Virginia countryside on a sunny crisp winter day. About half-way through our usual route along the Shenandoah River, he surprised me with the comment: "I think now may be a good time for you to take your [inner] life more seriously."
>
> Although the statement seemed quite accurate to me at the time, later I wondered why I had not reacted more defensively to it. After all, for almost two years I had been driving one and one-half hours each way, every six weeks or so, to see him. I really felt I had been investing good time and energy in being more open to the deeper elements in my life. So, my natural response could well have been: "Well, what do you think I have been doing?"
>
> However, I think the ideal timing and accuracy of his comment, as well as the trust I had in him and our relationship, made me see his words much differently. What I instantly felt he was trying to tell me was that it was time to leap more freely and deeply into what was truly important in life. (Wicks, 1997, p. 3)

More specifically, I think he meant that I needed to be involved in a threefold movement to be more clear as to: (1) the meaning that drove my work as a caregiver for other caregivers and what provided a theme and purpose for my personal life; (2) how I could continue to care for others in a professional yet deeply compassionate manner; and (3) how I could truly nurture my own interior life through creative, new, disciplined, and simple ways—what we might refer to here, in keeping with recent psychological and classic nontheistic approaches, as a sense of *mindfulness*.

Upon reflection, I recognized that to accomplish this, I would need to become more aware of the very things that I had encouraged in others. In other words, I would need to be honest and appreciate that:

- We get upset over too many things.
- Changes in one's life/schedule need not be seen only as disruptive.
- Quiet compulsions, rhythms, and resistances seem to rule more and more of our life, sapping it of its freshness.
- We increasingly use the "once this happens" (my children graduate from college, my challenging patients appreciate what I am trying to help them accomplish) philosophy of coping.
- There are increasing yearnings for and daydreaming about having more simplicity in our lives without taking any actions to achieve this.
- There is a large disconnect between the healthy way we treat our clients and the manner in which we treat ourselves.
- There is a failure to withdraw our projections and simultaneously touch all that we notice about ourselves— especially what we term "negative"—nonjudgmentally with compassion.

- A great deal of our time is spent either in the silver casket of nostalgia or fantasizing about the future.
- Time alone only seems to offer us a chance to ruminate, be resentful, worry, become discouraged, and feel lost, bored, or confused instead of providing the renewal that comes with some guidance on how to be mindful.
- An inordinate amount of time is wasted on the trivial (prestige, money, influence, fame, security, and pleasure) while the essential, simple joys of life are downplayed or elusive.
- Passion and commitment to what is really good and the awe and privilege of walking in life with people who are troubled but doing the best they really can have been replaced in some or many instances with attention only to the mechanics of treatment.
- A deep respect for patience and pacing has been replaced by a need to hurry, achieve, and "finally arrive" (whatever that means).
- Little potential mindfulness meditative periods (waiting in life, a cancellation of a session, a brief illness) are not accessed as spontaneous opportunities for the quiet, reflective, peaceful times they could be.
- An honoring of the rhythms of life seems absent and transitions only annoying.
- Time between patients or at the end of the day to reflect, debrief ourselves, and detoxify from all the negative and positive transferences is seen as a luxury given our full schedule and desire to quickly leave for home.

- The "ghosts" of our past when they intrude upon our peace and joy are not seen as "teachers" that carry valuable information for our growth.
- Periods of reflection fall prey to attitudes of arrogance (projection), ignorance (self-condemnation), or discouragement (the need for immediate gratification) rather than being filled with a spirit of intrigue about our gifts, growing edges, and resistances.
- Rather than prizing our gifts and seeing them as a pathway to serve others, we ignore them and hear praise as a whisper and negative feedback as thunder.
- The treatment we offer is no longer fresh; pat phrases and worn stories are the rule.
- Our health and love of life is often no longer infectious to our patients.
- We have very few activities in our lives that aren't competitive, for gain, add to our sense of security, or serve to medicate us.
- We have forgotten the major role of courage and transparency in both treatment and life.
- The desire to be truly sincere and respectful with ourselves has lost its greatness in our eyes.

Recognizing the importance of being aware of these points when and where they are valid for us can lead to a deeper and more resilient self. Yet, to my mind they would also require a broader awareness on our part of the aforementioned key approaches to the inner life. And, among them I believe that having an appreciation of the value of *silence* and *solitude* is especially important.

SILENCE AND SOLITUDE

The value of silence and solitude has recently been better recognized for its purely psychological worth due to the work of British psychiatrist Anthony Storr. In his classic work *On Solitude*, he notes:

> Modern psychotherapists, including myself, have taken as their criterion of emotional maturity the capacity of the individual to make mature relationships on equal terms. With few exceptions, psychotherapists have omitted to consider the fact that the capacity to be alone is also an aspect of emotional maturity. (1988, p. 18)

In this volume, he also presents Admiral Byrd as an example of someone who searched for solitude. Byrd appreciated the value of solitude as well as its offer of silence as part and parcel of his experience. Reflecting on his solo Antarctic expedition in the winter of 1934, Byrd wrote:

> Aside from the meteorological and auroral work, I had no important purposes. . . . Nothing whatsoever, except one man's desire to know that kind of experience to the full, to be by himself for a while and to taste peace and quiet and solitude long enough to find out how good they really are. . . . I wanted something more than just privacy in the geographical sense. I wanted to sink roots into some replenishing philosophy. . . . I did take away something that I had not fully possessed before: appreciation of the sheer beauty and miracle of being alive, and a humble set of

values. . . . Civilization has not altered my ideas. I live more simply now, and with more peace. (1958, pp. 7, 9, 62, 63)

A more recent publication in this area is *The Call of Solitude: Alonetime in a World of Attachment* by Buchholz, a psychologist. In it she echoes Storr's comments and the reflections of Byrd by writing: "We are born wanting and needing time and space alone to process the stimulation around us, as we also learn quickly to revel in and long for attached and related times" (p. 49). In this regard, she also refers to Thoreau's Walden Pond living experiment as follows:

Few in our society respect the sanctity of chosen alonetime. Even in a saucy book dedicated to fellow solitaires on how to make oneself company enough, author Barbara Holland mocks Henry David Thoreau's time to himself because he was never that far from human community. The point missed, however, is that, for a while, Thoreau chose to reverse the typical priority of people over solitude, *not* to abandon attachments. On July 4, 1845, Thoreau made his famous autonomous move to what he hoped would be the quiet of Walden Pond in Concord, Massachusetts. "Every morning was a cheerful invitation to make my life of equal simplicity and I may say innocence, with nature herself." He went there to examine his life and to seek protection from the contamination of industrial civilization. Thoreau and his friend Ralph Waldo Emerson believed in nature's healing powers and feared social demands as impositions that took people away from their true course in life. Yet neither man was antisocial or selfish. For example, both concerned themselves with the pursuit of people's rights and were against slavery. Walden Pond stands for a successful romantic retreat from the vicissitudes of everyday life perhaps because Thoreau also responded to his needs for engagement. (1997, pp. 190–191)

Psychologist Ellen Baker in her book on self-care for psychologists also addresses this same theme of solitude but with a very practical focus in mind:

Consciously building in self time at various points in the day is a valuable self-care practice. Ziegler and Kanas (1986) suggested that health care professionals "set aside an hour as 'inviolate' and relax, walk, run, meditate, or otherwise get it together" (p. 180). Despite a daunting work schedule, Zeiss (1996) spoke of her goal of continuing to set aside what she refers to as "sacred time" for herself and her psychologist husband on the weekend. . . . We can also borrow from religious and meditation practices. A tradition of "observing the quiet," in the service of connecting with one's self and the greater whole, is part of the Friends Quaker Society. (2003, p. 63)

CONTRIBUTIONS OF WORLD SPIRITUALITIES

As Baker recognizes, from a spiritual standpoint, long before Storr, Buchholz, and other psychiatrists and psychologists wrote positively about silence and solitude, all the major religions pointed out the value of taking out time to retreat from activity. This is continued in the writings of contemporary spiritual figures. For instance,

Henri Nouwen, a Catholic spiritual writer (and incidentally, also a psychologist), notes in his book *Way of the Heart* that silence and solitude are the furnace in which transformation takes place (Nouwen, 1981).

Contemporary Buddhist author Sogyal Rinpoche in his book, *The Tibetan Book of Living and Dying*, frames such periods of silence as "meditation." He points out that slowing down the pace of our lives by ensuring we have time to stop, breathe, slow down, and see how habits and compulsions have quietly strangled us is essential. He writes the following:

> We are already perfectly trained . . . trained to get jealous, trained to grasp, trained to be anxious and sad and desperate and greedy, trained to react angrily to whatever provokes us. We are trained . . . to such an extent that these negative emotions rise spontaneously, without our even trying to generate them. . . .
>
> However if we devote the mind in meditation to the task of freeing itself from illusions, we will find that with time, patience, discipline, and the right training, our mind will begin to unknot itself. (1992, p. 58)

He then goes on to say:

> The gift of learning to meditate is the greatest gift you can give yourself in this life. For it is only through meditation that you can understand the journey to discover your true nature, and so find the stability and confidence you will need to live, and die, well. . . . Our lives are lived in intense and anxious struggle, in a swirl of speed and aggression, in competing, grasping,

possessing, and achieving, forever burdening ourselves with extraneous activities and preoccupations. Meditation is the exact opposite. (Rinpoche, 1992, p. 57)

Orthodox Rabbi Aryeh Kaplan expresses a similar positive sentiment regarding meditation in his book *Meditation and Kabbalah*. He ties meditation to a number of sources, indicating the late eighteenth and early nineteenth centuries as its most popular period. He also acknowledges the fact that technique is similar throughout different world religions and points out that in Judaism there is a lack of awareness of this tradition of meditation for all practicing Jews:

With the spread of the Hasidic movement in the Eighteenth Century, a number of meditative techniques became more popular, especially those centered around the formal prayer service. This reached its zenith in the teachings of Rabbi Nachman of Breslov (1772–1810), who discusses meditation in considerable length. He developed a system that could be used by the masses, and it was primarily for this reason that Rabbi Nachman's teachings met with much harsh opposition.

One of the problems in discussing meditation, either in Hebrew or in English, is the fact that there exists only a very limited vocabulary with which to express the various "technical" terms. . . .

Many people [also] express surprise that the Jewish tradition contains a formal meditative system, that, at least in its outward manifestations, does resemble some of the Eastern systems. This resemblance was first noted in Zohar, which recognized the merit of the Eastern systems, but warned against their use.

The fact that different systems resemble each other is only a reflection on the veracity of the technique, which is primarily one of spiritual liberation. The fact that other religions make use of it is of no more consequence than the fact that they also engage in prayer and worship. This does not make Jewish worship and prayer any less meaningful or unique, and the same is true of meditation. It is basically a technique for releasing oneself from the bonds of one's physical nature. Where one goes from there depends upon the system used. (Kaplan, 1982, p. 3)

MINDFULNESS AND MEDITATION

Whether a person is not religious or is Buddhist, Muslim, Jewish, Christian, Hindu, or has another religious identity, the point made when we speak about time in silence and solitude or mindfulness meditation is that there is a benefit—especially for those of us who are clinicians. Mindfulness, which can be briefly defined as awareness of present experience with acceptance (Germer, Siegel, & Fulton, 2005, p. 7), offers us a milieu and approach for replenishing the self and maintaining perspective.

For instance, Clark Strand, a former Zen Buddhist monk, who wrote the book *The Wooden Bowl* about taking out time for meditation *even though you are no longer holding onto a religious or philosophical ideology*, noted:

All I wanted in the first place was to find the simple truth about who we are and how we ought to live. . . . I asked myself one question: Was there a way for people to slow down and experience themselves, their lives, and other people in the present moment. . . . The only thing [meditation] requires is that you be willing to remain a beginner, that you forgo achieving any expert status. . . . In other words, it requires you to maintain a spirit of lightness and friendliness with regard to what you are doing. It's nothing special, but it works. (1988, pp. 2–3)

In extolling the value of being mindful, he goes on to say what he believes it offers all of us:

Perhaps you have had the experience of waking well-rested on a Saturday morning. Your mind is alert but you have not yet begun to think about the day. The sun is shining in the yard and all around you is perfectly clear morning light. That alertness sustains itself without even trying. You may not even notice it except for the feeling of being rested and ready for the day.

The experience of meditation is something like that. When you meditate you are not trying to have any particular experience. You are simply awake. After having counted your breath from one to four for several minutes, quite without having aimed at that experience, you start to feel a kind of clarity and space surrounding each number as you count. It feels a little like having enough space to think, enough room to move and breathe, or simply "be." (Strand, 1998, p. 96)

Still, the questions remain as to how we do it. What is the cost involved in terms of time and loss of illusions about ourselves and the benefits that are possible so we can consider the effort worthwhile? By this I mean:

We must be able to hear our own inner voice instead of only our anxieties and the myriad fearful and negative voices that fill our outer world at home, in the classroom, at places of amusement, [in private practice,] and that even dominate our places of worship! But in today's active life, where and when do we find such space? Furthermore, given our lack of experience with it, how will we spend this time alone in a way that is renewing? We don't want to let it be just a time for moody introspection or vengeful musings about how we have been mistreated in life. . . .

The benefits are certainly there if we approach such a place, not with a sense of duty, but as a time for returning to our self; it will become a gentle place of reassurance, reassessment and peace. Time spent in silence and solitude on a regular basis can effect us in the following ways:

Sharpen our sense of clarity about the life we are
    living and the choices we are making;
Enhance our attitude of simplicity;
Increase our humility and help us avoid unneces-
    sary arrogance by allowing time to examine the
    defenses and games we play (these often surface
    for us to see during quiet times);
Let us enjoy our relationship with ourselves more;
Decrease our dependence on the reinforcement of
    others;

Enable us to recognize our own areas of anger, enti-
   tlement, greed, cowardice (given the opportunity
   to quietly review the day's activities and our
   reaction to them);

Protect our own inner fire so that we can reach out
   without being pulled down;

Help us accept change and loss;

Make us more sensitive to the compulsions in our
   lives;

Experience the importance of love and acceptance (which are fruits of the contemplative life)
   and acknowledge the silliness and waste involved
   in condemning self and judging others;

Allow us to hear the gentle inner voice that reflects
   the spiritual sound of authenticity . . . and

Help us respect the need to take time to strengthen
   our own inner space so that we can, in turn, be
   more sensitive to the . . . presence of others. . . .

In other words, taking quiet time in solitude and silence
during each day can provide us with a place to breathe
deeply. . . . Yet, even when we know the true value of silence
and solitude, we often run from it. For us, to value the quiet in
our lives, we must know not only what these periods can do
for us but also . . . be able to really appreciate *what price they
may extract from us.* Otherwise, we will just continue to speak
about silence and solitude wistfully as something wonderful
and never enjoy what this well of truth and support can offer
us. (Wicks, 1998, pp. 41–43)

RECOGNIZING THE CHALLENGES OF SILENCE, SOLITUDE, AND MINDFULNESS

People always make time for what they want to do. When their schedule is full, they may get up early, stay up late, or set aside periods during the day—even if it turns out to limit their lunch break. So why would we not want to set aside time for quiet periods if we feel they really have so many benefits?

Resistance to Solitude

Silence speaks eloquently in solitude; listening quietly to our hearts allows us to walk unprotected and unguarded with the Truth in our inner "garden." However, this time of quiet listening may also present us with a challenge: It may bring us to a place of loneliness and vulnerability, open us to a new recognition of hidden lies. So, although the process of taking time away from our daily activities is essential and good, there are elements with which we will find it difficult to deal once we embrace silence and solitude. We should know about this challenging reality so that the unconscious hesitancy to take quiet time doesn't surprise us and totally undermine our efforts to seek solitude. Time away for reflection is too valuable to lose because of ignorance or hidden anxiety.

Our natural tendency is to actively avoid silence and time alone. Distracting and amusing ourselves with activities is a much more common practice than being involved on a regular basis in the process of reflection. . . . [It] confronts us with the awkward way we often live out our days; likewise, in silence, we are reminded of our mortality. Consequently, talking about [mindfulness] is a lot easier than [meditating].

Thus, when we seek to establish a life of reflection or further develop the . . . life [of silence and solitude] we have, we must realize that the process won't go as smoothly as we'd like. A road sign at the beginning of a highway construction site outside of Washington, D.C., warns: BE PREPARED TO BE FRUSTRATED!

As we travel along the roadway of [meditation], the same advice is often appropriate. The difficult experiences we encounter during periods of solitude need not be considered negative even if initially we feel that they are. If we neither avoid nor run away from them, we can learn to understand and appreciate the constructive moments of our periods of loneliness, vulnerability and discovery.

For instance, a number of years ago, as I was walking down a winding Virginia road with my mentor, I shared with him an unusual experience I had during my quiet time. I said to him, "My life is basically quite good. I don't feel deprived or needy. Instead, most of the time I feel grateful and challenged. However, lately in my quiet time of reflection, I have felt a sense of wistful loneliness, like something was missing. I felt a light ache of emptiness passing through my stomach . . . that something real, important and basic was missing, and I deeply yearned for it—whatever this 'it' was."

His response surprised me. He did not brush off my experience as of no consequence, advise that it would pass shortly or tell me how to combat it. Instead he said, "That's good. The loneliness that you describe is meant to remind you that your heart will not be ultimately satisfied by anyone or anything now in this life. Your loneliness also reminds you that even though you may distract yourself with many things and people—even lovely ones—your sense of being at home can only be given by something deeper, greater.

"And so, the loneliness will allow you to enjoy people, things and life in general *in their proper perspective*. As a result, you can enjoy the people and gifts in life, but they will not become idols for you because your loneliness will teach you. . . .

"Then, rather than being tempted to 'set up tents' prematurely when you have wonderful experiences or relationships, you will have the freedom to enjoy them without being captured and controlled by your desire for them. Therefore, the loneliness will keep your heart open, aware; your journey will continue with a sense of passion and expectancy. That is, if you let it and don't try to avoid or 'medicate' such initially troubling feelings with activities, distractions or work."

Andrew Harvey, in his famous book *A Journey in Ladakh*, approaches this feeling from a Buddhist perspective by offering a response he received from someone with whom he shared a similar situation:

> As we parted, he hugged me and said, "You smile a great deal and you listen well, but I see that somewhere you are sad. I see nothing has satisfied you. . . ."
>
> I started to protest.
>
> "No," he said, "nothing has satisfied you, not your work, not your friendships, not all your learning and traveling. And that is good. You are ready to learn something new. Your sadness has made you empty; your sadness has made you open!" . . .

A Psychological Vacuum

As well as opening us to loneliness and vulnerability, silence and solitude can form a psychological vacuum into which many feelings, memories and awarenesses (which lie just below the surface in the preconscious) may be encouraged to surface. At such times as these, we are being called in reflection . . . to face the truths about ourselves that for some unconscious reason we may have put aside, denied or diminished.

Having such truths surface is not terrible, of course, especially if we remember that many of these insights will actually be helpful rather than harmful. The only "damage" is that which will be suffered by the false image of ourselves that we have created because we haven't been willing to trust in our own inherent value. So by spending time in silence and solitude, we will be able to see the extent to which our self-worth has, to this point, been built upon a foundation of sand. We will come to recognize that our sense of self-worth is dependent in an exaggerated way on praise by others, positive experiences we have (including ones in prayer and meditation) and a list of other past achievements. Though unpleasant, finding out this truth is still quite life-giving. Such an epiphany allows us to rediscover a sense of self and worth grounded in true self-respect. We then can come to understand that real self-respect is based on a deep, concrete trust in the inherent spiritual value of being a human person rather than on specific accomplishments or the reception of kudos from others.

Arriving at this point of insight is not a magical process. The desire to be a person who is solidly aware of self-worth no matter what others say or do, no matter what mistakes or shameful things we might do, cannot thrive just as a wishful thought. It has to be welcomed and passionately sought in silence and solitude, that place in which a strong and healthy attitude toward *all* of life is formed. (Wicks, 1998, pp. 45–49)

Once we consider taking out the time to sit in silence and solitude or are involved in a mindfulness meditation in a group, we may then come up with another set of objections.

The *first objection* is: "When I quiet down and try to enjoy the silence, all I do is hear the noise of my thoughts and worries. So I know I'm not made for meditation or reflection." This is a typical objection of beginners. It needs to be handled, otherwise we will quit after a couple of minutes, no matter how many times we try.

The reality is that most of us hear noise in our minds all day long. When we sit in silence the first important bit of information we get is to learn how preoccupied we are with so many things. Knowing this is helpful because it:

- Helps us let the static expend itself. (Given a chance, after a while our mind calms down);
- Gives us some indication of the type of worries we have about which we feel helpless or anxious. (We get a chance to hear what we are continually thinking);
- Prepares us to empty our minds so we can breathe deeply, relax, and experience "the now" rather than always being caught in the past or preoccupied with the future.

So, expecting the noise and letting it move through us are two ways we can meet the objection that we are not suited or able to quietly reflect or meditate. The reality we must remember is: Many people with our personality type have found meditation wonderfully helpful. It is not just for a certain type of person.

A *second objection* is: "Meditation or reflection is too hard and alien. I'm not a yogi and have found meditation or even quiet prayer uncomfortable." The response to this is simple:

- Find a quiet place (alone if possible).
- Sit up straight.
- Close your eyes or keep them slightly open looking a few feet in front of you.
- Count slow, naturally exhaled breaths from one to four and repeat the process.
- Relax and let stray thoughts move through you like a slow-moving train, repeating themes; observe objectively then let them go. . . .
- Experience living in the now.

A *third objection* comes in the form of a question: "What will this time do for me? I'm a busy person and time is too precious for me to deal with impractical exercises." There are many responses to this. For our purposes here—namely, the desire to change, grow, and be more free—the following are especially relevant:

- When we are quiet we are able to experience all of the pulls, anxieties, and conditioned responses we have going on all day but may fail to notice. So, at the very least it informs us of the nature of the blocks we have to feeling at ease, flexible, open, and ready to change when necessary.

- Not only will we be able to see what absorbs us but how things we didn't realize have become our most important reference point or center of psychological/spiritual gravity.
- Once we have this information we can take note of it and reflect on it mentally, in journaling, or with a mentor during other periods outside of the quiet time.
- Also, the peaceful times when we sit and reflect physically stop us from running, running, running, without taking a breath, and so experience what it means to be alive and, in the process, ask ourselves if that is where we want to focus our lives.

If it sounds like I'm putting great emphasis on quiet time, I am. I have found if we give some space to ourselves and try not to judge ourselves/others harshly, avoid panicking or trying to immediately solve a problem, but instead calm ourselves down, we will learn not to jump to quick conclusions; our usual ways of doing business (our programming) will not take over. This will allow our habits to loosen their hold on us so we can see life—including ourselves—differently.

When people do express their gratitude for my recommendation that they take at least two minutes a day for quiet reflection first thing in the morning, they often report extending it to twenty minutes. Then they try to find another ten minutes during the day to reconnect with the experience and find another few minutes in the evening to become tranquil, give closure, and release the day before they go to sleep.

In guiding others toward using meditation as a building block to enable change, one of the other things I also notice is that it loosens people up throughout their whole day—not just during the reflection period. The more we allow our thoughts to inform, rather than frighten, depress, or anger us, the less we are grasped by our [rigid] thinking and inter-pretations. We are not in a vise but are instead free to use our power of observation, analysis, and curiosity to help us learn valuable lessons about life. Meditation not only frees us to be open during the period of reflection, it also produces an attitude that makes us less defensive and more intrigued with stumbles as well as triumphs. It can positively contaminate our day! (Wicks, 2000, pp. 52–55)

LISTENING AND REFLECTION: CORNERSTONES OF MINDFULNESS

Listening to the people around us and opening ourselves to what we hear coming from within us may cause us some shame and emotional pain at first, if we are really honest. However, just as we should not turn our back on others who would help us see the truth, we must also have the patience and fortitude to "just sit" and be quiet when all that comes from within rises to the surface. As Achaan Chah advises:

> Just go into the room and put one chair in the center. Take the one seat in the center of the room, open the doors and windows, and see who comes to visit. You will witness all kinds of scenes and actors, all kinds of temptations and stories, everything imaginable. Your only job is to stay in your seat. You will see it all arise and pass, and out of this wisdom and understanding will come. (Quoted in Kornfield, 1993, p. 31)

By having a listening spirit, we recognize that we must face things directly. The American Buddhist nun Pema Chodron addresses this issue in her book *When Things Fall Apart*. She writes:

> The trick is to keep exploring and not bail out, even when we find out something is not what we thought . . . [a] sign of health is that we don't become undone by fear and trembling, but we take it as a message that it's time to stop struggling and look directly at what's threatening us. (1997, p. 5)

Being as open as we can in both meditation and our relationships can teach us a great deal about ourselves if we really listen

(a very important word) to the people and the world around us . . .

   "and by opening" . . . ourselves (despite the pain that may be associated with it) to the possibilities . . . that fill and surround us and sometimes . . . even come kicking, scratching, or begging at our door. (Wicks, 1997, p. 14)

And so, what we are speaking about here in the effort to be a true listener to whatever provides greater awareness and inner strength is not something to be taken lightly. To put it another way:

The interior life then is not an imaginary or psychotic world. It is not a place to run to so we can pout, brood, fantasize revenge, or to ruminate over things as a way to mentally beat ourselves up. Instead, as we have seen it is a place of self-knowledge, self-nurturance, challenge, and solid peace. It is a place that will not only be our strength but also one that we can offer to others. When our interior life is strong, our attitude toward others is gentle. When our inner life feels nourished, our hearts can be open to others' pain.

In a reflection on our time together, one person whom I journeyed with said: "And what will I leave behind from our relationship: my 'stuckness,' my unconsciousness, my shame and guilt, my repressed pain, resentment and depression. . . . And what will I take with me? What will be awakened through the gift of our relationship? My playfulness, my love of life, my sense of wonder, my gratitude, my openness, and my wholeness."

Unfortunately, though, our inner life is often infected by some of the negative "atmosphere" of our upbringing. For instance, Gorky (1996) in his autobiography said: "Grandfather's house was filled with a choking fog of mutual hostility. It poisoned the grown-ups and even infected the children." (Gorky, 1996, p. 173)

Our response to such influences is to build a persona inside that is filled with fear, hesitancy, prickliness, and anger—not a very gentle place for us to center ourselves. Moreover, when our inner life is narrow and distorted, our understanding, appreciation, and grasp of life also suffer dramatically. Carl Jung, the famous Swiss psychiatrist, put it in these terms:

> People become neurotic when they content themselves with inadequate or wrong answers to the question of life. They seek position, marriage, reputation, outward success or money, and remain unhappy and neurotic even when they have attained what they were seeking. Such people are usually confined within too narrow a spiritual horizon. . . . If they are enabled to develop more spacious personalities, the neurosis generally disappears.

What he is speaking about here is the inner life . . . the one we all long for as a way of finding a deep well within ourselves which will remain calm and pure no matter how stormy, violent, or polluted the interpersonal "weather" around us becomes. The inner life is important because it impacts every aspect of our living since we interpret all aspects of life via this inner sense of self and the world. For instance, one person who was sexually abused at a very young age said at the end of therapy that, early in her life, transitions seemed abrupt, fearful, and everything seemed worse after them. "Now that I am in a different place in my heart," she said, "transitions are to be reached out to with wonder and awe."

The state of our interior life *does* make a difference to others. When we have a gentle, healthy, and strong inner life, we are part of the healing stillness in the world which offers places of hope to all who suffer and yearn for justice, solace, and encouragement. But if we, like so many others, do not feel at home within ourselves, and by ourselves, we will then add to the sense in the world that nowhere is there a safe and good place.

This is a very dangerous situation not only for us but also for the young who follow and try to model themselves after us. Ten years ago one pediatrician noted to me that she saw the light go out in the eyes of many fifth and sixth graders—now she sees this same sad shroud over their spontaneity in the second and third grades.

So, we need to build our inner life. (Wicks, 1997, pp. 14–16)

Such a building process involves a number of factors with which we must be familiar.

Being a listening-reflective person does take some sense of structured intention rather than just motivation and good will. As well as time in silence and solitude for mindfulness meditation in which there is no agenda, it also involves the following elements of a reflective period at a certain point in the day and/or week:

1. Establishing a time to reflect;
2. Selecting meaningful events in our day and life to reflect upon;
3. Entering those events by reliving them in our minds;
4. Given our desires, goals, and philosophy of life, to learn what we can from these events;
5. Enlivening the learning through action.

What such a Structured Listening-Reflective Exercise might involve are:

Time: A little time is needed to reflect on one's day. If we rush through life without thought we will know it. One sign we are doing this is the statement: "Where did the time go?" When our life is passing like a blur it doesn't mean we live very active lives. What it does show is that we are leading busy lives. The difference between active and busy is the former includes reflection and is directed, whereas the busy life feels out of control and does not seem purposeful or meaningful.

Select: To make our reflection useful and not just a time to preoccupy ourselves, worry, or let our mind wander, we should pick out specific events or interactions during the day that caused a significant reaction.

Enter: Then we should put ourselves back into the events so we can relive them. This time as we experience it we can observe our reactions, note them, and see what themes or understanding we can glean. (Remember, don't blame others or condemn self, just neutrally observe and seek to analyze.)

Learn: Given what we understand and what our core beliefs (psychological or spiritual) are about life, what did we learn from this reflection? Often when we have values, we can see how we followed those values or ignored them.

Action: Finally, learning is only important when it changes the way we live. How we will act on our new learning is essential. And it can't be action that is immature, such as making the vow, "*I'll never trust him again!*" when you feel a person has let you down. Instead, using the example just cited, you must see what about the interaction led you to be naive and put more trust in a certain person than he/she could bear. So, in other words, action must be based on insight that we have about our *own* behavior, beliefs, and thoughts. Otherwise, the results will be just a sophisticated form of pouting, projecting, and avoidance of self-understanding. (Wicks, 2000, pp. 57–58)

When we become true mindful listeners, we practice being people who recognize that there are many voices calling to us of which we are not aware. The sources of these voices may be good in their own way and include: the desire to succeed, be well off financially, be admired, be spectacularly effective, or be loved. The sources can be career, family upbringing, society, the health care system, politics, or culture. The important thing when we make daily decisions and ones that impact us in the long run is to know which one(s) are primary at any given time so we more clearly decide based on this knowledge as to what we wish to do in any given situation. One of the positive outcomes of a strong "inner life" is an improved level of self-awareness (which will be the focus of the next chapter). However, beyond this, for therapists, mindfulness can improve their overall quality of life.

MINDFULNESS AND THERAPIST WELL-BEING

As Brazier points out:

The therapist is concerned with the quality of the client's life moment by moment. . . . Therapy is more about improving the quality of life than solving specific choice dilemmas. Improving life quality begins with mindfulness.

Meditation has been used for millennia to cultivate the mind. . . . Although there are many different approaches, all involve quieting habitual energies: cleansing perception so that we can see what is going on. Mindfulness is an attempt to regain contact with the flow of experience.

Mindfulness is both radical introspection and direct connection with the phenomenal world. It is not simply inward looking. It is more a matter of being fully present in each step of life. . . . Simple degrees of mindfulness are immensely valuable, indeed essential at all levels of personal growth. (1995, p. 73)

However, such a process of development that is enhanced by mindfulness is not restricted, nor obviously should it be, to our clients. In therapy (to quote Brazier again):

However we do it, creating a conducive space is important. . . . It is fairly easy to create a safe space of sorts by creating an outside enemy and this temptation is always there in therapy. . . . The therapists, therefore, empty themselves so as to have room for the client to fill them. It is our own emptiness which begins the therapeutic process. . . . I, therefore, find it enormously helpful to have a short period of quiet sitting before my client arrives. Even a few minutes of meditation helps me become calm and grounded. . . . When the therapists have space within themselves, then they can be at one with anybody. (1995, pp. 22–24, 28)

Poetically, Kornfield echoes this theme indicating that through mindfulness

we allow ourselves the space of kindness. There is beauty in the ordinary. We invite the heart to sit on the front porch and experience from a place of rest the inevitable comings and goings of emotions and events, the struggles and successes of the world. (1993, p. 208)

Accomplishing this on a basic level involves some simple steps. Cozolino in his book *The Making of a Therapist: A Practical Guide for the Inner Journey* recognizes the obvious reality that when a therapist is frenetic, no good can come of it; therefore, he suggests the five following basic strategies to help therapists stay centered:

- Allow extra time to get to your office so you don't arrive anxious or tense.
- Think of the 5 minutes before each session as a time to get relaxed and centered.
- Schedule breaks during the day for rest, reading, or social contacts.
- Don't overbook your week—avoid emotional and physical exhaustion.
- Monitor your emotional and physical state and adjust your schedule when needed. (2004, p. 19)

These are all initial steps that can enhance balance. Yet, there is much more to be gained for therapists in having a more pervasive sense of mindfulness in their lives. Germer, in the opening chapter to the benchmark book on the topic—*Mindfulness and Psychotherapy*—that he, Siegel, and Fulton edited, from a different, broader angle, also notes:

Therapists may be drawn to mindfulness for the simple reason that they would like to enjoy their work more fully. Psychotherapists choose to witness and share human conflict and despair many of their waking hours. Sometimes we are asked by a sympathetic patient, "How do you do it?" What *do* we do when a clinical situation appears impossible to handle? How do we stay calm and think clearly?

Doing psychotherapy is an opportunity to practice mindfulness in everyday life. The therapy office can be like a meditation room in which we invite our moment-to-moment experience to become known to us, openly and wholeheartedly. As the therapist learns to identify and disentangle from his or her own conditioned patterns of thought and feeling that arise in the therapy relationship, the patient may discover the same emotional freedom. The reverse is also true; we can be moved and inspired by our patients' capacity for mindfulness under especially trying circumstances.

Practicing clinicians are reminded regularly about the importance of the therapy relationship in treatment outcome. . . . When focused primarily on implementing an empirically derived protocol, to the exclusion of a vital, interesting, and supportive therapy relationship, therapists and their patients can both lose interest in the work. In the coming years, mindfulness practice may prove to be a tangible means for building empirically supported relationship skills. This may help return our focus to the therapeutic connection, since there is something we can *do* to improve it. How we plan interventions may even be guided by a common therapeutic principle—the simple mechanism of mindfulness. (2005, p. 12)

Mindfulness meditation practices that can help therapists both work with their patients and themselves were given a major advance with the emergence of Jon Kabat-Zinn's work. His development of Mindfulness-Based Stress Reduction (MBSR) at the University of Massachusetts Medical Center's Stress Reduction Clinic demonstrated both in his intensive training and his books (see selected bibliography) that mindfulness *can be learned*.

MINDFULNESS CAN BE LEARNED

During a workshop sponsored by Harvard Medical School on "Mindfulness and Psychotherapy," a psychiatrist whispered a question to me during one of the breaks. He asked: "Everyone here seems to have a mindfulness practice? Do you?" Implicit in his question was, "Where does one begin in developing such a practice? It seems so overwhelming and elusive."

Here it may help to gather some basic answers to this very question and concern about the seeming elusiveness of mindfulness:

- Take at least a few minutes in silence and solitude each morning to center yourself. Do this by selecting a quiet place, sitting up straight, and simply counting your breaths from one to four while allowing whatever thoughts that arise to pass through you without suppressing or entertaining them;

- Ensure you have breaks between patients or groups of patients to quiet and separate yourself from what you have experienced so you decontaminate yourself of the stressful elements of intensive encounters you have as a clinician;
- Be faithful to the self-care protocol you have developed as a result of encountering the material presented in chapter 2 of this book;
- Ensure you take a brief walk at least once during the day;
- Provide time for the *Structured Listening Reflective Exercise* previously described in this chapter;
- Outline and practice the five basic strategies to help clinicians stay centered that were described by Cozolino; and finally—and possibly of greatest import with respect to reinforcing all of the above steps,
- Read, reflect upon, and practice exercises and principles you feel appropriate that are included in the books from the selected bibliography on mindfulness.

As Germer aptly recognizes:

> Any exercise that alerts us to the present moment with acceptance cultivates mindfulness. Examples are directing attention to one's breathing, listening to ambient sounds in the environment, paying attention to our posture at a given moment, labeling feelings, and so forth. The list is endless. (2005, Germer, Siegel, & Fulton, p. 14)

The question in response to this comment may be, "Am I not doing that now?" The response that this past chapter has attempted to offer to this question is: Yes, but qualitatively you can live in a more mindful way with a bit more attention, some structure, and a little more awareness of what experienced practitioners have to teach us. As Weiss notes in his book *Beginning Mindfulness*:

> Meditation is not just something you do on a cushion or chair. Anything you do is an occasion to engage yourself mindfully in the present moment. . . . Ultimately, the path of mindfulness will lead you to a place within yourself where you may encounter the world without ideas or preconceptions, where you can disengage from your habitual narrative and free yourself from mental constructs . . . [and it] gives us a way through suffering to joy. (2004, p. xvii)

If any person or profession would benefit from mindfulness given this description of potential results, certainly it has to be today's involved clinician.

Psychiatrist Arthur Deikmann in reflecting on the life and teachings of Shunryu Suzuki (whose books on mindfulness—*Zen Mind, Beginner's Mind*, and *Not Always So*—are classics), said, "Where he is is where I want to be . . . in that place of sanity" (Chadwick, 1999, p. 313). To be in such a place ourselves requires attention, time, desire, and some guidance.

At the end of this book, there is a selected bibliography on mindfulness. By way of closing this chapter, though, I offer several quotes from just three of them: Andrew Weiss's *Beginning Mindfulness* (2004), Bhante Henepola Gunaratana's *Mindfulness*

(2002), and the nationally acclaimed book by Jon Kabat-Zinn, *Wherever You Go, There You Are: Mindfulness Meditation in Everyday Life* (1994). The first two authors provide simple advice on the process of mindfulness and, I believe, reinforce well that mindfulness can indeed be learned. They provide some simple building blocks of mindfulness that can be used immediately while reading further in this area in books that were prepared by experienced guides and are listed in the selected bibliography at the end of this book. The final quote from Jon Kabat-Zinn is a call to wake up now; it is, to my mind, one of the most simple, yet compelling, statements on the importance of living a mindful life I have ever read:

Andrew Weiss

Mindfulness practice comes in two varieties: formal and informal. The formal practice is what we would normally call "meditation," for which we set aside a specific time to sit silently with mindful awareness of our breathing, or to walk slowly and silently with mindful awareness of our breath and our walking. The informal practice involves mindfulness of our daily-life activities, and is just as much "meditation" as the formal practices are (Weiss, 2004, p. 3).

Mindful meditation . . . is about waking up. We spend most of our lives caught up in the conceptual knowledge we have acquired, and in our concepts of who we are, or what our lives mean, or what a tree is or what a boulder is, and so on and on. This layer of concept sits between us and the reality of the present moment. . . . To allow this layer to drop away we first have to be able to stop (Weiss, 2004, pp. 4, 5).

Here are some possible ways to reinforce mindfulness in
your daily life . . .

- When you wake up in the morning, allow yourself
  some slow, mindful breaths before you get out of bed.
- Try eating breakfast without reading the newspaper
  or watching television. If possible, eat silently for all
  or part of your meal. Before you eat, allow yourself
  to breathe in and out three times and bring your
  awareness to the food in front of you.
- Take a few minutes, either at home or on your way
  to work, to notice something enjoyable about the
  morning. . . .
- On your way to work or school, or to appointments
  or your other daily errands, try to be mindful of
  your traveling. . . .
- Several times during the day allow yourself to
  become aware of your breathing and re-center
  yourself. . . .
- Many things happen every day that you can use as
  bells of mindfulness: the door bell, the telephone,
  sounds on your computer, turning on a light. . . . Let
  each one be an occasion to notice your breathing
  and allow some mindful in-and-out breaths. . . .
- If you work on a computer, create a screen saver
  that encourages mindfulness—perhaps a photo of
  flowers or animals. . . .
- During your lunchtime, allow yourself some enjoyable time in addition to your meal. Talk with a
  friend, perhaps, or take a walk. . . .

- When you are ready to leave your day's activities, take a moment to appreciate what you've done that day. . . .
- Help to make your trip home a transition time by slowing down. . . . Allow your attention to be with your surroundings. . . .
- As you go to bed and prepare for sleep, take some mindful breaths, become aware of the bed supporting you, and allow yourself a smile. (Weiss, 2004, pp. 13–18)

Bhante Henepola Gunaratana

The process of meditation is extremely delicate, and the result depends absolutely on the state of mind of the meditator. The following attitudes are essential to success in practice . . . :

1. *Don't expect anything.* Just sit back and see what happens.
2. *Don't strain.* Don't force anything or make grand, exaggerated efforts. . . .
3. *Don't rush.* There's no hurry, so take your time.
4. *Don't cling to anything, and don't reject anything.* Let come what comes. . . . Don't fight with what you experience, just observe it all mindfully.
5. *Let go.* Learn to flow with all the changes that come up. . . .
6. *Accept everything that arises.* Accept your feelings, even the ones you wish you didn't have. . . .

7. *Be gentle with yourself* . . . You may not be perfect but you are all you've got to work with. . . .

8. *Investigate yourself.* Question everything . . . The entire practice hinges upon this desire to be awake to the truth.

9. *View all problems as challenges.* Look upon negatives that arise as opportunities to learn and grow. . . .

10. *Don't ponder.* You don't need to figure everything out. Discursive thinking won't free you from the trap. In meditation, the mind is purified naturally by mindfulness, by wordless bare attention.

11. *Don't dwell upon contrasts.* Differences do exist between people, but dwelling upon them is a dangerous process. Unless carefully handled, this leads directly to egotism. (Gunaratana, 2002, pp. 39–42)

Jon Kabat-Zinn

If what happens now does influence what happens next, then doesn't it make sense to look around a bit from time to time so that you are more in touch with what is happening now, so that you can take your inner and outer bearings and perceive with clarity the path that you are actually on and the direction in which you are going? If you do so, maybe you will be in a better position to chart a course for yourself that is truer to your inner being—a soul path, a path with heart, *your* path with a capital P. If not, the sheer momentum of your unconsciousness in this moment just colors the next moment. The days, months, and years quickly go by unnoticed, unused, unappreciated.

It is all too easy to remain on something of a fog-enshrouded, slippery slope right into our graves; or, in the fog-dispelling clarity which on occasion precedes the moment of death, to wake up and realize that what we had thought all those years about how life was to be lived and what was important were at best unexamined half-truths based on fear or ignorance, only our own life-limiting ideas, and not the truth or the way our life had to be at all.

No one else can do this job of waking up for us, although our family and friends do sometimes try desperately to get through to us, to help us see more clearly or break out of our own blindnesses. But waking up is ultimately something that each one of us can only do for ourselves. When it comes down to it, wherever *you* go, there *you* are. It's *your* life that is unfolding. (Kabat-Zinn, 1994, pp. xvi, xvii)

CHAPTER FOUR

Daily Debriefing

*Mindfulness and Positive Psychology
as an Integral Part of the Clinician's
Ongoing Self-Reflective Process*

I believe that the highest success in living and the
deepest emotional satisfaction come from building
and using your signature strengths.

—Martin Seligman, *Authentic Happiness*

All effective therapists intuitively find a way to
capitalize on the strengths of their characters. Freud's
self-analytic skills, Roger's genuineness, Ellis's
capacity for rational thinking, Perl's playfulness,
formed a nucleus for their respective theories. So,
too, do clinicians translate their inner selves into a
personal style of helping.

—Jeffrey Kottler, *On Being a Therapist*

If acute and chronic secondary stress are to be limited and one's
personal and professional well-being are to be enhanced, then self-
knowledge and the enlightened behavior that it should give rise to

are not a nicety in clinical practice; they must be a given. Personal discipline and self-management are essential parts of clinical practice. This is referred to as "self-regulation." In her book on self-care, Baker writes, "*Self-regulation*, a term used in both behavioral and dynamic psychology, refers to the conscious and less conscious management of our physical and emotional impulses, drives and anxieties" (2003, p. 15). She then goes on to warn:

> Managing our affect, stimulation, and energy as we navigate our professional and personal lives, as well as our relationships with self and others, is no easy task. To regulate mood and affect, we must learn how to both proactively, constructively manage dysphoric affect (such as anxiety and depression) and adaptively defuse or "metabolize" intense, charged emotional experience to lessen the risk of becoming emotionally flooded and overwhelmed. However, as Coster and Schwebel point out, if we are to "manage" ourselves or "regulate" our behavior, obviously sound self-awareness must be present (Coster & Schwebel, 1997, p. 10). Nowhere is this more necessary than in the clinical setting. (Baker, 2003, p. 15)

It is very easy to lose one's way—even from the very beginning of one's journey in professional mental health—unless something or someone helps us gain perspective. Harvard psychiatrist Robert Coles, in reflecting on his years in medical school, shares a story that aptly illustrates this:

> I was in medical school in Columbia and not enjoying it much. Kept complaining about it to my mother, and she said that what I needed was to go down and work at a [New York

City] soup kitchen for Dorothy Day instead of complaining.
I understood what my mother was getting at. She used to
say that there are things more important than the troubles
you're having, and there are people who might help you to
understand that and especially help you to get some distance
from your complaining and from the rather privileged position of being a medical student. The long and short of it is,
I eventually went down there and met Dorothy Day. (Cole,
2003, quoted in R. Riegle, p. 140)

Unfortunately, this problem doesn't end with graduation. Loss
of perspective remains a danger all through one's career if time
isn't taken to reflect on our personal and professional lives. The
following anecdote on how easy it was for a seasoned neurologist
to lose a sense of what was important illustrates this well. He dem-
onstrates, like Cole did, that sometimes even when you are dealing
with life and death on a daily basis, it takes someone from your
circle of friends or family to remind you how quickly all of us can
blow things out of proportion when we don't take time out to reflect on our feelings, thoughts, beliefs, and behavior:

The following letter, written by a first-year college student to
her father during the middle of her second semester, delight-
fully points [out how easy it is to lose perspective no matter
how delicate and important one's work is.] Prior to receiving
this note, her father was totally preoccupied with her "success" in college. He was worried because she didn't do well in
her first semester and was concerned she would fail out during the second semester—and take his money with her! He
had forgotten, as many of us parents do, that performance in

courses is only a partial measure of learning; moreover, there is much more to the total college experience than just grades.

Despite her youth, this woman knew this better than he, and so taught him an important lesson on perspective. On the front page of her note it said:

> Dear Dad,
>
> Everything is going well here at college this semester, so you can stop worrying. I am very, very happy now . . . you would love Ichabod. He is a wonderful, wonderful man and our first three months of marriage have been blissful.
>
> And more good news Dad. The drug rehab program we are both in just told us that the twins that are due soon will not be addicted at birth.

Having read this, her father then turned the page with trepidation. On the other side of the note it said:

> Now, Dad, there actually is no Ichabod. I'm not married nor pregnant. And I haven't ever abused drugs. But I did get a "D" in chemistry, so keep things in perspective! (Wicks, 1992, p. 115)

It is very easy to move through life—even the most service-oriented of lives—in such a compulsive, driven way that we feel out of control. When we take out time to reflect on who we are and what we are doing we often see how "unfree" we have become in so many ways. In his most classic work, physician and Russian spiritual leader Anthony Bloom puts it in a way that is easy to image:

> There is a passage in Dickens' *Pickwick Papers* which is a very good description of my life and probably also of your

lives. Pickwick goes to the club. He hires a cab and on the way he asks innumerable questions. Among the questions, he says, "Tell me, how is it possible that such a mean and miserable horse can drive such a big and heavy cab?" The cabbie replies "It's not a question of the horse, Sir, it's a question of the wheels," and Mr. Pickwick says, "What do you mean?" The cabbie answers, "You see, we have a magnificent pair of wheels which are so well oiled that it is enough for the horse to stir a little for the wheels to begin to turn and then the poor horse must run for its life." (1970, p. 39)

Bloom then adds by way of commentary on this: "Take the way we live most of the time. We are not the horse that pulls, we are the horse that runs away from the cab in fear of its life" (Bloom, 1970, p. 39). The bottom line is: You can count on losing perspective and deluding yourself if time is not devoted to reflection on your thoughts, behavior, and affects. But it isn't easy to be honest with yourself.

Zen master Shunryu Suzuki once cautioned his students: "When you are fooled by something else, the damage will not be so big. But when you are fooled by yourself, it is fatal" (Suzuki, as cited in Chadwick, 1999, p. 308). In a book on the dynamics of being a woman physician, the author wrote, "What's good about medicine is that there is always something to do, so you don't have the time to think about your problem." Then, she added: "What's bad about medicine is that there's always something to do, so you don't have the time to think about your problems *enough*." The same, I think, can be said about social work, counseling, and psychotherapy.

Real self-knowledge can even be elusive for those who are professionals dedicated to helping others achieve new degrees of clarity about their lives. Donald Brazier reflects this reality in a book advocating the use of an integration of Zen with psychotherapy when he notes:

> These days . . . we are apt to seek out a therapist to . . . help us get the dragon back into its cave. Therapists of many schools will oblige in this, and we will thus be returned to what Freud called "ordinary unhappiness" and, temporarily, heave a sigh of relief, our repressions working smoothly once again. Zen, by contrast, offers dragon-riding lessons, for the few who are sufficiently intrepid. (1995, p. 14)

Given the personal psychological dangers to clinicians themselves (as well as their patients) when they are not self-aware, social workers, psychologists, counselors, and other mental health professionals must be among those who are "the sufficiently intrepid" with respect to their self-awareness. To deal with this, simple "self-mentoring approaches" offer a structure for the type of ongoing reflective process that is a *sine qua non* of being a clinician.

UNIQUENESS AND SELF-KNOWLEDGE

No matter what approach is used to understand stress—be it weighted in the direction of environment or personality—the individual is naturally always a factor. This is observable in persons who come in for psychiatric or psychological treatment. I have found that "a significant turning point in therapy or counseling arrives when the individual seeking help is able to grasp the following, simple, seemingly paradoxical reality: When we truly accept our limits, the opportunity for personal growth and development is almost limitless. Prior to achieving this insight, energy is wasted on running away from the self, or running to another image of self" (Wicks, 1986, p. 5). Such obviously is the case with most of us who are clinicians as well.

This should not be surprising since recognition of this reality is reflected in the writings of nonclinicians as well. Poets, theologians, and great scientists have joined those in the mental health field to warn people not to be unconsciously pulled into trying to be someone you are not. In the words of e. e. cummings, for example, "To be nobody but yourself in a world which is doing its best, night and day, to make you everybody else—means to fight the hardest battle which any human being can fight, and never stop fighting" (Wicks, 1986, p. 5). Jewish theologian Martin Buber (1966) echoed this same theme from a slightly different angle by noting the following story to illustrate it:

> The Rabbi Zusya said a short time before his death, "In the world to come, I shall not be asked, 'Why were you not Moses?' Instead, I shall be asked, 'Why were you not Zusya?'"
> (Wicks, 1986, p. 6)

The point being made is that it can be a great struggle to be "simply ourselves"—especially when we are in a transferential role such as psychotherapist, counselor, or social worker where people are turning to us when they are vulnerable much in the way they turned to parents and significant figures from their past. This can't be prevented, but in terms of our own sense of self, we must be constantly aware that this perception is based on their needs and personality and not on our abilities or objective reality. Being "extra-ordinary" is not being a super person, as some (including, unfortunately, us and some of our colleagues at times) would want to believe. Instead, it is being self-aware and in tune with the way our talents and the needs of those we work with in mental health and social work act in synchronicity. Accomplished inventor and global citizen R. Buckminster Fuller phrased it this way in terms of the dangerous lures he met during his own life:

> The only important thing about me is that I am an average healthy human being. All the things I've been able to do, any human being, or anyone, or you, could do equally or better. I was able to accomplish what I did by refusing to be hooked on a game of life that had nothing to do with the way the universe was going. I was just a throwaway who was willing to commit myself to what needed to be done. (Buckminster Fuller, as cited in Wicks, 1986, p. 6)

Having a view such as that of Buckminster Fuller takes a degree of humility. Yet, with such humility, not only do mental health professionals avoid the unnecessary stress that comes from living as if the transferences put on them by patients are in fact a reality, but it also helps the students whom seasoned practitioners are called to guide. As Pfifferling in a discussion of medical education indicates in a way that has direct relevance for those of us who have completed training as psychotherapists, counselors, and social workers:

> Students can be exposed to the mistakes made by their faculty so that error in problem solving can improve learner behavior. Faculty self-disclosing behavior and modeling of personal/ professional humility to a student, reinforce the necessity to

be on guard against medical arrogance that can cost a patient his life. By self-disclosing mistakes to their students, the faculty prevent the student from becoming too arrogant or too distanced from the troubles of their patients, and provider/patient bonding is strengthened and improved. (1986, p. 14)

Full self-awareness that includes such an awareness of our emotional sensitivity or lack of it is very elusive. In the words of poet Henry David Thoreau, "It is as hard to see oneself as to look backwards without turning round" (Thoreau, as cited in Auden, 1976, p. ix). Yet, every effort must be made to increase self-understanding—not just to curb our errors but to increase our own self-respect because as Leech aptly notes, "You do not want to know someone whom you despise, even if, especially if, that someone is you" (Leech, 1980, pp. 43–44). One feeds the other and forms a positive circle. Self-respect is really true self-awareness.

To become clearer about ourselves, there is a need to expend energy, but it obviously helps to know the most productive and efficient way to do this. To best accomplish a sense of clarity about our feelings, beliefs, and actions, appreciating the value of discipline, noting inconsistencies and exaggerated emotions, and avoiding vagueness (a sign that the defense of unconscious repression is at work) would be helpful.

EMBARKING ON A DISCIPLINED SEARCH

Self-awareness is an ongoing, dynamic undertaking that requires daily attention. When we have such a process in place, we can become more attuned to the rhythm of our personality and have our "psychological fingers" on the pulse of where we are emotionally with respect to an issue, person, challenge, or the general thrust of where our life is moving.

To accomplish this, we need to be aware of the ebb and flow of our reactions so we can become more sensitive to the subtle inconsistencies in our affect (e.g., experiences of sadness, depression, happiness, etc.), cognitions (ways of thinking, perceiving, and understanding), and actions. This provides us with a link to some of the motivations and mental agendas that lie just beyond our awareness—what some would refer to as our "preconscious" or unexamined schemata (beliefs). To be in a position for such an appreciation of ourselves, time must be taken to identify anything in the way we live that is incongruent so we can seek to understand the reason for the difference.

Instead, what often happens when we do, think, or feel something that is generally out of character for us is that we dismiss it as irrelevant or excuse it ("I was just tired, that is all"). However, when we do this and do not seek to accomplish a creative synthesis in understanding all parts of ourselves, we will miss the normally buried treasures in our psyche that provide clues to material that is generally not available to us for consideration.

ELEMENTS OF CLARITY

One of the constants present when mental health professionals seek help to avoid or limit the sources and symptoms of secondary stress is the temporary lack of clarity they are experiencing. In mentoring, the goal is to help them to clarify, discern different approaches, and problem solve solutions to their inner and external stresses. To accomplish this, time must be taken to focus on the specifics of their reactions. This helps the person to move through conscious (suppression) and unconscious/preconscious (repression) avoidance or forgetting. As in the case of our clients or patients, by limiting vagueness and a tendency to generalize or gloss over details and feelings, information that lies just beyond our sense of awareness becomes available. So, rather than turning away from the seemingly unacceptable feelings, cognitions, impulses, and reactions, we face the anxieties that they produce as a price for learning more about ourselves. The benefit, of course, is greater self-knowledge and, in turn, more personal freedom. Rather than being limited by our blind spots in self-awareness and the waste of energy on defensiveness, by focusing on our interactions during the day we seek to become sensitive to *all* of our reactions—even the seemingly incongruous ones—as a way to deepen our self-knowledge. This is especially important for us, because as clinicians we are required to interact at times with clients who, while doing their best given difficult early parenting, may still be very challenging.

One of the reasons people resist complete clarity in life is that it can't be limited only to how others (e.g., our patients, their families, or colleagues) are stymied in denial. We also must look at our *own* behavior, cognitions, and affect. Clarity is a process by which we must be willing to look at how we are also denying, minimizing, rationalizing, or hiding things from ourselves. Although we often say that we want to see ourselves and our situation as they truly are, conflict often arises when this happens because the responsibility then falls on us to:

- Be aware of all of our own agendas—including the immature ones
- See our own defensiveness as well as our tendencies to project blame onto others

- Find appropriate levels of intimacy with those with whom we interact
- Know how to deal with anger and our unhelpful reactions to failure
- Achieve a level of skill as a critical thinker
- See the crucial role of positive psychology in enhancing the paradigm of clinician self-awareness.

AWARENESS OF ALL OUR AGENDAS

Thinking that we do things for only one reason is naive. In most cases, there are a number of reasons—some immature, some mature—that we do things. Since the ones we don't like to acknowledge tend to remain beyond our awareness, clarity calls on us to uncover and take creative efforts to embrace all of them. In this way, through awareness the chances will increase that the immature reasons can atrophy and the mature ones can grow and deepen. However, to accomplish this goal, we must first accept that we are all defensive in some unique way. Such an admission is an excellent first beginning because it doesn't put us in the position of asking: "Are we or aren't we?" Instead, it moves us out of the black-and-white situation to the gray areas where most of us psychologically live. When we look at all the reasons that we reacted to a situation in the way we did, we can begin to appreciate why people react to us in the way that they do. Otherwise, we will remain puzzled, feel misunderstood, and project all the blame outward so as never to learn what the dynamics are and how to unravel them in any given situation.

For instance, if colleagues don't like to work with us in stressful situations, it would be helpful for us to know our part in it so we can work on decreasing the incidence of it. Once a candidate applying for a position as my assistant when I was chair of a counseling program asked me, "Do you know how human resources is billing the main challenge of working with you?" Surprised—after all, how could there be *any* challenge in working with me—I responded, "No, I don't." To which she noted with a smile, "They are billing you as a perfectionist who gives vague instructions and gets upset when they are not followed exactly." Impatience, anger, and other reactions on our part don't increase efficiency when we are working with colleagues in a difficult clinical emergency. Blaming our reactions solely on other people's incompetence provides very limited information for improving the situation by changing our own behavior. Reacting emotionally in a way that makes the situation deteriorate further certainly doesn't improve things either.

Clarity calls on us to recognize our agendas, face our own fears, understand the games we play with others, lessen our defensiveness, develop new coping skills, and create alternative ways to deal with stressful situations. Yet to do this, we have to be honest. We also have to appreciate that this can have a positive domino effect in our life as a way of moving through the resistances we have to growth and change. When we start focusing on understanding individual interactions, larger questions open up as to whether we as clinicians are getting enough rest or leisure, the right balance of time alone and with good friends, and how and when we are setting limits in all aspects of our lives. It is important to recognize that the self is a limited entity that can be depleted if we don't involve ourselves seriously in a process of self-care that includes self-knowledge. Through simple, periodic self-questioning (see appendix F), we can better see our motivations, fears, and interpersonal style more clearly. The more this is accomplished, the more we will almost automatically withdraw our projections, take control of our lives, and—in the process—reduce unnecessary secondary stress. The problem is that as clinicians we take for granted that we do this as a matter of course. Unfortunately, with busy schedules, such time for structured self-awareness often isn't undertaken as often and regularly as it should be. This can develop into a real problem—especially when we are confronted with failures, as we certainly will be, given the intense nature of our work with people experiencing serious psychological, medical, and social difficulties in such a stressful, uncertain world.

FACING FAILURE IN A PRODUCTIVE WAY

A reality in social work and mental health is that the more you are involved with persons who are suffering, the more you are going to fail. So, you'd better be able to put failure in perspective. The myth that if one is up on the literature, pays attention to the client or patient, provides an accurate diagnosis and regimen of treatment, then failure is impossible, is very destructive to the spirit of the clinician. Failure is part and parcel of involvement. Given the many demands and the inability to be perfectly "on" all the time, failure will occur. However, although this is inevitable when we are constantly dealing with people with psychological, physical, and social needs, failure can still provide helpful information. It can limit future mistakes and provide insight into how people in the clients' interpersonal environments experience and react to them. In fact, if we look carefully at our clinical work, failure can actually teach us to:

- Recognize the dangers of pride and the need for openness
- Consider ways to avoid errors in the future
- Change factors that increase the possibility of failure
- Experiment with new approaches
- Learn about ourselves
- Improve technique and collaborative style
- Be sensitive to early warning signs of mistakes
- Consider the impact of negligence
- Uncover areas where further education/supervision is required
- Appreciate unrealistic expectations
- Improve pacing in one's work
- Acknowledge personal/professional limitations so ones that can be corrected or improved will be and we will be more aware of the limitations that are more or less permanent or characterological in nature.

If failure is carefully considered rather than just allowed to become a source of self-condemnation or an impetus to blame, deny, or distort the situation, present and future patients will benefit immeasurably from the process of examination on our part. However, to accomplish this, as clinicians we must seek to be critical thinkers.

CRITICAL THINKING

Critical thinking helps us understand situations, clients, and colleagues, as well as our own agendas, negative emotions, attitudes, motivations, talents, and growing edges more clearly. This helps us not only have a greater grasp of reality but also stops the drain of psychological energy it takes to be defensive or protect our image. Since critical thinking is not natural—although we may think it is for us—it takes discipline, a willingness to face the unpleasant, and a stamina that allows us not to become unduly frustrated when we don't achieve results as quickly as we'd prefer with respect to our own insights and growth.

As clinicians, the types of questions we must be willing to ask ourselves as critical thinkers are:

- Am I willing to avoid seeing things simply in black-and-white and entertain the various aspects and ambiguity in life?
- Can I appreciate that the "answer" or diagnosis I now offer is always tentative?
- When I am in a discussion of a patient, clinical situation, or even my own role, talents, and growing edges as a professional and a person, am I able to entertain the possible as well as the probable without undue discomfort?
- Do I need to come to a quick solution or take one side of an issue because I lack the intellectual stamina that encourages an open mind?
- Am I so uncomfortable with personal rejection, a tarnished image, or failure that I capitulate when I disagree with others?

- Am I willing to "unlearn" what I have learned that is not useful anymore and be open to new techniques and approaches?
- Do I realize that I resist changes in obvious and less noticeable ways and that one of my goals is to see my emotions and extreme reactions as red flags that can often indicate that I may be holding on because of fear, stubbornness, or some other defensive reason?

The willingness to be a critical thinker and face questions like the ones above takes not only motivation but also involves an appreciation of how resistant most of us are much of the time without even knowing it.

APPRECIATING AND OVERCOMING OUR OWN RESISTANCE TO CHANGE

Change—even when we are aware that we have problems that need to be confronted—sometimes seems so elusive. As F. Robert Rodman, in his classic work on becoming a psychotherapist, *Keeping Hope Alive*, notes:

> Every patient stared at long enough, listened to hard enough, yields up a child arrived at from somewhere else, caught up in a confused life, trying to do the right thing, whatever that might be, and doing the wrong thing instead. (1985, p. 5)

However, this point obviously does not only hold for persons seeking counseling and psychotherapy. Clinicians need to recognize their own resistances as well. Yet, even when they are motivated to do so, this is sometimes easier said than done.

As Thomas Merton, contemplative and author of the classic autobiographical work *The Seven Storey Mountain*, laments:

> All day I have been uncomfortably aware of the wrong that is in me. The useless burden of pride I condemn myself to carry, and all that comes with carrying it. I know I deceive myself . . . but I cannot catch myself in the act. I do not see exactly where the deception lies. (1988, p. 161)

Understanding as much as we can about our own hesitancy to both uncover resistances and act effectively to address those areas we need to change is essential. This is especially so if you are a mental health or social work professional where stress is so intense and working through resistances can literally be the difference between life and death, burning out or not, living with meaning or drifting in quiet blunted despair.

How we in the helping professions understand and address the concept of "resistance" in helping patients who are experiencing emotional distress has changed over the years. And so, a quick review of this concept is helpful as a professional update as well as for clinicians wishing to overcome their own barriers to personal and professional growth:

> In the early years of psychology, a client's resistance to change was often looked upon as solely a *motivational* problem. When a person did not succeed in changing, the counselor felt: "I did my job in pointing out your difficulties. In return, you didn't do yours!" The blame rested upon the one seeking

change. The goal was to eliminate the resistances and get the person motivated again.

Now, we recognize that when someone resists change and growth in their personal and professional lives they are not purposely giving family, friends, coworkers and counselors a hard time. Instead, they are unconsciously providing a great deal of critical information on problematic areas of their life given their personality style, history, and current situation. This material then becomes a real source of new wisdom for psychological growth, professional advancement, and spiritual insight.

Though we still believe motivation is an essential key to making progress, we see that persons seeking change must also gain certain knowledge about themselves and act on it if they wish to advance. Or in a nutshell: *Motivation or positive thinking is good, but it is obviously not enough.* (Wicks, 2000, p. 9)

As clinicians, we know that one of the primary reasons that motivation to change is not a sufficient condition for the alteration of one's attitude, cognition, and behavior is that we fear that the demands of change may be too costly. For instance, we would have to see our own role in the problems we are having and do something about it. In addition, we worry about how other people will react when we seek to move away from defensiveness or unhealthy competitiveness. The move toward health is also surprisingly upsetting to those who are used to "the devil they know" with his or her defensive style. It might even challenge them to change, and they would be uncomfortable in dealing with this. Finally, seeing our own role in our problems does cause some negative reflection about the past and how much time we have wasted in behaving as we have. Despite such resistances to insight and growth, the "advantages" of staying the same are very costly and the freedom and insight change offers both us and our clients are so great. Consequently, with respect to the tyranny of habit and secondary gain, we must take whatever measures we can to make our steps toward self-knowledge and personal-professional growth more realistic. So, as in the case of our approach to those we treat, two ways we can improve our own self-awareness are by increasing our sensitivity to our defensiveness and taking what actions we can to outflank our resistances.

INCREASING SENSITIVITY TO RESISTANCES
TO CHANGE AND OUTFLANKING THEM

When we seek to export the blame for problems in our life as clinicians, we refer to it as "projection." This defensive style is manifested in many obvious and quiet ways. They include: denying our role in mistakes or failures, excusing our behavior, contextualizing our actions, absolving ourselves for ignoring or crossing boundaries, rationalizing failures, and generally removing ourselves from the equation while focusing on the negative roles others have played.

We do this partly in reaction to a general tendency to go overboard when trying to take responsibility for our own role in various unpalatable events. Instead of trying to understand what part we played so we can learn from this, we move from remorse about what we've done to shame about who we are. With this movement from remorse to shame, we start to condemn ourselves, become hypercritical of our behavior, overly perfectionistic, unrealistic in our comparison with others in the field, and overresponsible with respect to the impact we did and can have.

A better approach is to recognize and act upon the need to take a step back from the event, try to frame the situation in an objective way by almost behaving as if it involved someone else, and seek to become intrigued about our role. In this way, we increase the possibility for change. At the same time, we are more likely to avoid overly blaming others, condemning ourselves, or getting discouraged when results don't happen immediately. Accordingly, in a spirit of mindfulness and to further reduce the resistance to change, there are several caveats I normally offer in order to outflank the blocks to growth in myself and others. They are:

1. Anything discovered does not have to be changed immediately;
2. No area should be condemned . . . just neutrally observed as if it were happening to someone else;
3. No area should be defended—no one is criticizing or attacking, just observing where the energy is being spent;
4. Observations—even disturbing ones—should be embraced as a wonderful treasure trove of information;
5. After each period of observation, the areas of concern should be written down so some record is kept of discovery. (Wicks, 2000, pp. 70–71)

With these provisions in mind, persons can then consider the following principle:

Where there is energy (positive or negative) there is usually a grasping and/or fear. When the smoke of a strong reaction is present, the fire of desire is also usually present and we need to know what it is. Otherwise, rather than our passions being good energy, they may be the product of unexamined attachments. (Wicks, 2000, p. 71)

They then keep us connected to views and convictions that are covering or distorting the truth rather than leading us to it. Classic signs that we are holding on include: arguing, not sharing all the information or motivations with persons with whom we discuss the event, complaining that change in certain areas is un-realistic, stonewalling persons through an icy silence or monopolizing the situation, feeling misunderstood or totally ignored, and other strong emotions or off-putting actions.

On the other hand, there are also classic signs that a person does value change, growth, and insight both professionally and personally. Some of these signs are:

- An ability to let go
- Receptive to new lessons . . .
- Not self-righteous
- Intrigue with one's own emotional flashing lights
- Disgust with . . . the endless wheel of suffering that comes from grasping and bad habits
- Curious, not judgmental
- Values experience
- Recognizes danger of preferences which prevent experiencing new gifts in life
- Awake to present; is mindful
- Appreciates quiet meditation
- Generous and alive

- Learns, reflects, and applies wisdom to daily life
- Rests lightly in life. (Wicks, 2000, pp. 78–79)

In recognizing and overcoming resistances to growth and change, then, we are able to appreciate that the most important person in improving our situation is *ourselves*. As clinicians, we accept this responsibility not with a spirit of self-condemnation or overresponsibility but with a sense of intrigue about the possibility within ourselves. We can see that at times we are emotional and opinionated. We understand that blindness like this occurs because of fear and hesitation that may be partially rooted in our past but is certainly centered in a belief system that is tyrannical and often wrong. This results in a style of "self-talk" that comes as our friend and seemingly supports us. Nevertheless, in the end, it undercuts our ability to see things clearly and have solid self-esteem. Such clarity and self-esteem must be rooted in a kind of honest self-knowledge that allows us to view with equanimity our talents and gifts as well as our growing edges.

IMPROVING SELF-TALK

One of the main contributions of cognitive-behavioral psychological theory is its ability to help people better appreciate how our beliefs (schemata) and cognitions (ways of thinking, perceiving, and understanding) can impact the way we feel and behave. Unfortunately, as therapists, counselors, and social workers, we learn that dysfunctional ways of perceiving ourselves and the world are common and often left unchallenged. Such inattention is psychologically dangerous—especially if you are a clinician.

A number of years ago, in line with the work of seminal thinker Aaron Beck, psychiatrist David Burns in his popular book *Feeling Good* illustrated how people fall prey to cognitive errors that may lead to depression and/or an overall sense of discouragement. Perfectionistic clinicians are in particular danger of such irrational thinking if they are not aware of it. Among Burns's categories, worth reviewing again after all these years with an eye to how we, as clinicians, commit these common errors, are:

ALL OR NOTHING THINKING: You see things in black-and-white categories. If your performance falls short of perfect, you see yourself as a total failure. . . . OVERGENERALIZATION: You see a single negative event as a never-ending pattern of defeat. . . . MENTAL FILTER: You pick out a single negative detail and dwell on it exclusively so that your vision of all reality becomes darkened, like the drop of ink that discolors the entire beaker of water. . . . DISQUALIFY THE POSITIVE: You reject positive experiences by insisting that they "don't count" for some reason or other. In this way you can maintain a negative belief that is contradicted by your everyday experiences. . . . EMOTIONAL REASONING: You assume that your negative emotions necessarily reflect the way things are: "I feel it, therefore it must be true . . ." SHOULD STATEMENTS: You try to motivate yourself with should and shouldn'ts. . . . The emotional consequence is guilt. When you direct should statements toward others, you feel anger, frustration, and resentment. . . . PERSONALIZATION: You see yourself as the cause of some negative external event which in fact you were not primarily responsible for. (1980, pp. 40–41)

For me, the core of the issue here is that:

Negative thinking is quite common. For some reason, all of us seem to give more credence to the negative than to the positive. We can hear numerous positive things but somehow allow a few negative things to discolor and disqualify the previously affirming feedback we received. Therefore, we need to (1) pick up and recognize our negative thinking so we can (2) link the negative thoughts we have to the depressive/anxious feeling we experience, so (3) the negative self-talk we have can be replaced with a more realistic thought or belief. It is in this way that we structure changing our negative thinking so our negative beliefs can eventually be modified as well.

We can always—and, unfortunately, frequently do—find a negative comparison to make when we are reflecting on our thoughts, actions, and motivations. . . . Making negative comparisons between our situations and those of others is never a problem. Maintaining perspective . . . is the difficulty!

We may say we already know this but can't seem to put it into practice. When I hear this statement I think of Mark Twain's comment: "The difference between the right word and the almost right word is the difference between lightning and the lightning bug." We may say we know it, but unless we can truly recognize and short-circuit the negativity that causes insecurity [and] increases defensiveness . . . then we really don't know it. (Wicks, 1988, pp. 30–31)

As Rainer Maria Rilke wrote in his classic work *Letters to a Young Poet*:

> Only someone who is ready for everything, who excludes nothing, not even the most enigmatical, will live the relation to another as something alive and will himself draw exhaustively from his own existence. For if we think of this existence of the individual as a larger or smaller room, it appears evident that most people learn to know only one corner of their room, a place by the window, a strip of floor on which they will walk up and down. Thus they have a certain security. And yet what dangerous insecurity is so much more human which drives the prisoner in Poe's stories to feel out the shapes of their horrible dungeons and not be strangers to the unspeakable terror of their abode. We, however, are not prisoners. No traps or snares are set about us, and there is nothing which should intimidate or worry us. . . . We have no reason to mistrust our world, for it is not against us. Has it terrors, they are *our* terrors; has it abysses, those abysses belong to us; are dangers at hand, we must try to love them. (1954/2004, pp. 68–69)

The issue once again is: the way we perceive something is just as relevant as what we perceive. Only when we realize this, then can we see that both successes and failures can be used to increase self-understanding and self-appreciation. This is so much more life giving than seeing our successes and failures only as a constant see-saw of ups and downs in our life and in our work. When we recognize this, how we look at or question ourselves changes dramatically, as do our overall results.

Self-understanding, not self-indictment, is at the basis of the self-questioning process. This is important to reflect upon again and again—especially when we are conducting a systematic self-evaluation of ourselves, our stresses, and the personal and professional goals we have. In addition to having this nonjudgmental attitude when interviewing ourselves, a *structured* approach might be helpful so we don't avoid or miss areas. When we interview ourselves in an effort to uncover cognitive and affectual styles, the chances are great that we may miss or unconsciously avoid some area. Therefore, in the discerning process of improving self-awareness, a basic questionnaire (see appendix F) accompanied by a basic interpretation guide (appendix G) is provided to spur comprehensive self-reflection. However, before this, a discussion of how positive psychology might help clinicians—rather than just clients—to look at themselves in a more balanced way is offered.

POSITIVE PSYCHOLOGY AND CLINICIAN
SELF-AWARENESS

For most of the history of clinical psychology (and possibly to a somewhat lesser extent in the case of clinical social work and counseling), the focus has been on ameliorating suffering through primarily being concerned with the *negative* side of personality and distress. Little was done with deepening the fine aspects of a person's life. However, energy is now being expended by a number of researchers to provide additional areas of emphases in how we approach people in today's stressful world.

According to Martin Seligman, who initiated the positive psychology movement and in the process counterbalanced the medical model's sole focus on pathology:

> The field of positive psychology at the subjective level is about positive subjective experience: well-being and satisfaction (past); flow, joy, the sensual pleasures, and happiness (present); and constructive cognitions about the future—optimism, hope, and faith. At the individual level it is about positive personal traits—the capacity for love and vocation, courage, interpersonal skill, aesthetic sensibility, perseverance, forgiveness, originality, future-mindedness, high talent, and wisdom. . . . Psychology is not just the study of disease, weakness, and damage; it also is the study of strength and virtue. Treatment is not just fixing what is wrong; it also is building what is right. . . . the major strides in prevention have largely come from a perspective focused on systematically building competency, not correcting weakness. . . . This, then, is the general stance of positive psychology toward prevention. It claims that there is a set of buffers against psychopathology: the positive human traits. (2002, pp. 3–7)

In a broad sense, Seligman is also concerned that the tendency when looking at behavior is to interpret even the positive actions people take as being the result of compensations and defenses rather than to see them in a positive light. He refers to this as the "rotten to the core doctrine" and provides a wonderful illustration of this in his popular, helpful book *Authentic Happiness*:

> The rotten-to-the-core doctrine also pervades the understanding of human nature in the arts and social sciences.

Just one example of thousands is *No Ordinary Time*, a gripping history of Franklin and Eleanor Roosevelt written by Doris Kearns Goodwin, one of the great living political scientists. Musing on the question of why Eleanor dedicated so much of her life to helping people who were black, poor, or disabled, Goodwin decides that it was "to compensate for her mother's narcissism and her father's alcoholism." Nowhere does Goodwin consider the possibility that deep down, Eleanor Roosevelt was pursuing virtue. Motivations like exercising fairness or pursuing duty are ruled out as fundamental: there *must* be some covert, negative motivation that underpins goodness if the analysis is to be academically respectable.

I cannot say this too strongly . . . there is not a shred of evidence that strength and virtue are derived from negative motivation. (2002, pp. x, xi)

His findings and that of other researchers in the positive psychology area are important in how we mold treatment approaches. It is also important, in terms of the focus of this book, in how clinicians view themselves professionally and personally.

For instance, theories on why persons desire to become clinicians has traditionally included such negative motivations and traits as:

- Compensating for the clinician's own childhood experiences;
- A desire for an ego boost or control;
- A fulfilling of the need to have persons depend on them;
- A narcissistic need to be the center of a person's life.

Sussman (1992), in his book *A Curious Calling: Unconscious Motivations for Practicing Psychotherapy*, fleshes out these theories even more clearly. However, as in the case of Seligman's viewing the behavior of Eleanor Roosevelt as pursuing virtue, why not view the positive possibilities for persons' becoming clinicians and give them credence as well? These might logically include:

- A desire to be helpful;
- True empathy and concern for people suffering;
- A desire to make a difference in the world;
- Commitment to expanding an important field of knowledge;
- A sense of joy at helping others maximize their potential.

It seems that for a long time we have more readily accepted as realistic that clinicians, "down deep," entered the field for defensive reasons and not positive ones. As Seligman and other researchers in this area note, the unfortunate part of this is that this claim has until recently remained unchallenged, unproven, yet tacitly accepted.

Yet, even more important than appreciating the positive reasons for entering and staying in the clinical arena, for our purposes in this book, it is also essential to have clinicians look at themselves in a different, more complete way when debriefing themselves at the end of a day or undertaking an informal self-reflection at the end of the work week so resiliency is encouraged rather than torn down. "Countertransferences" and "compensations" in a clinician's work and personal life may indeed be realities to profitably examine, but it is just as, maybe even more, essential to look at one's signature strengths and therapeutic talents as well.

This needs to be done on an ongoing basis because as Seligman notes, building on what is right about a person is one of the best ways to strengthen and enhance potential. Certainly this relates to clinicians as much as anyone else. As Morgan notes in terms of mindfulness of intention:

> In the first therapy session, we typically inquire about precipitants, problems, and pain. Often we neglect to ask about deeper intentions, desires, and values:
>
> - "What is your heart's desire?"
> - "What is truly important to you?"
> - "How do you most want to live?" (2005, p. 148)

In line with the spirit and intent of positive psychology, such a wonderful approach with clients is certainly no less useful in the case of those of us who treat them.

To accomplish this in the most complete way possible, the reader is referred to the selected bibliography on positive psychology in this book. In addition, at the end of this chapter, questionnaire 4.1 is provided on the theme *Positive Psychology and Clinician Self-Questioning/Reflection*. In reviewing these questions, the goal for clinicians is to balance the tendency to look *solely* at their shortcomings and mistakes (as essential as this may be) with an appreciation of how their talents and gifts are also in play. This is undertaken to balance and enhance interpretations of the past and present motivations and actions as well as to instill a greater sense of optimism and hope in one's personal life and professional work. The rationale is that, potentially, this more balanced attitude toward debriefing may turn out to be the most significant part of the reflective process undertaken during the day, week, month, year, and periodic life span changes one moves through. Moreover, as we will see below, positive emotions can expand the repertoire of our approach to our clients and our own personal life.

Several points made by Peterson—in what I have found to be one of the most engaging, succinct, yet complete introductions to the area (*A Primer in Positive Psychology*)—will set the stage for considering the questionnaire (4.1). According to Peterson:

> **Positive psychology** is the scientific study of what goes right in life. . . . It is a newly christened approach within psychology that takes seriously as a subject matter those things that make life worth living . . . positive psychology does not deny the valleys. Its signature premise is more nuanced but nonetheless important: What is good about life is as genuine as what is bad and therefore deserves equal attention from psychologists. (2006, pp. 4, 6)

The field of positive psychology provides a framework for examination of the "good life," as Peterson also writes:

> We can parse the field into three related topics: (a) positive subjective experiences (happiness, pleasure, gratification, fulfillment), (b) positive individual traits (strengths of character, talents, interests, values), and (c) positive institutions (families, schools, businesses, communities, societies). (2006, p. 20)

In addition to a focus on a client's assets, positive psychology also investigates the ways healthy organizations contribute to mental health (Seligman, 2002).

In her theories of mental health, Barbara Fredrickson emphasizes that positive and negative emotions work differently. Peterson points this out as follows:

Negative emotions alert us to danger. When we experience a negative emotion, our response options narrow, and we act with haste to avoid whatever danger is signaled. In contrast, positive emotions signal safety, and our inherent response to them is not to narrow our options but to broaden and build upon them. The evolutionary payoff of positive emotions is therefore not in the here and now but in the future. Perhaps it is advantageous to experience positive emotions because they lead us to engage in activities that add to our behavioral and cognitive repertoires. (2006, p. 58)

For our purposes in this book, the above raises a question beyond client care; namely, if we see that positive psychology's findings may result in an adjustment of our view with respect to how we can help clients live their lives more fully, should we not also be concerned as well about helping ourselves as clinicians in this way? More specifically, after sessions, should it only be the countertransferences and mistakes that we seek to uncover and reflect upon to improve our work, or should we also note what went *right* in the session. Should we seek to enhance our therapeutic gifts and talents as well as limit our errors? Furthermore, in our personal and professional life beyond the consulting room, should we not take into consideration as well how we are already living life fully and seek to enhance it even more? Doesn't this make more sense than just taking note of the stresses so we can avoid unnecessary burnout or vicarious PTSD, as important as this may be?

In reflecting on the work of Csikszentmihalyi (2000) and what this leading positive psychology researcher/author wrote in his well-received book *Flow*, Peterson also adds that flow describes a psychological state of being that accompanies attention-consuming activities. In order to experience flow, there must be an ideal balance of skill already possessed and challenge encountered. If an activity is either too difficult or too simple, flow does not result. As our ability to accomplish an activity increases, so does the opportunity to experience flow. Once an individual discovers his or her most rewarding activities, it is important for him or her to add those activities to his or her life regularly (Peterson, 2006).

This is but a sample of the way this broad field is being approached by different researchers. The particular approach just mentioned—"flow theory"—also is especially relevant for clinicians in terms of their own self-understanding and self-care. The balance of skill and challenge can lead to such helpful questions for psychotherapists, counselors, and social workers as:

1. With what type of clinical situations do I seem to lose track of time?
2. What challenges would I want more of in my clinical practice?
3. What are some of the skills that would help me feel less under stress in my work with clients?
4. With what type of clients do I seem to know exactly what to do and to feel most helpful, given my talents and gifts?
5. When do I worry the most about what other professionals will think about me? What can I do to lessen this?

6. What experiences do I enjoy the most professionally? Why is this so, and what can I do to expand the possibility of their happening?
7. What type of clients/client problems are: below my skill level? even with my skill level? above my skill level?
8. How am I dealing with the above levels?
9. What types of clinical situations do I really find intrinsically motivating and why?

In line with this, other related positive psychology themes such as gratitude, optimism, and hope are also important areas to reflect upon. They are noted in the books included in the selected bibliography on positive psychology, are the driving force behind some of the questions in the questionnaire with which this chapter is concluded, and are noted briefly in the epilogue, which is to follow. The primary goal, though, is to provide a reflective grid that not only focuses on areas to improve upon but also those experiences, events, behaviors, cognitions, gifts, talents, and conditions to be recalled, celebrated, and reinforced. Such an approach, whether conscious or not, needs to be included in a rich work/life style inventory for resilient clinicians. Not to do so may very well lead to courting discouragement, an imbalanced self-view, a locus of control outside of oneself, and ultimately unnecessary secondary stress. That is why incorporating positive psychology along with mindfulness approaches in the clinician's self-care/self-awareness process is essential.

With the above in mind, this chapter is closed with a questionnaire designed to encourage clinicians to consider how positive psychology might provide them with insights into their *own* behaviors, cognitions, and style of living as well as how they are practicing social work, counseling, or psychotherapy. While the questions, in and of themselves, can enable clinicians to entertain making changes based on new insights, it is my hope that reflecting on them will also encourage reading further in Seligman, Peterson, Csikszentmihalyi, Boldt, Joseph and Linley (who provide a meta-theory for clinical practice in their book *Positive Psychology*), and the other professional works on the topic in the selected bibliography. Certainly, making such reading and reflection a part of the professional/personal renewal activities in one's self-care protocol over the next year would be congruent with enhancing the resiliency and role and life enrichment that is being encouraged here.

QUESTIONNAIRE 4.1

Positive Psychology and Clinician
Self-Questioning/Reflection

There are a number of Web sites (e.g., authentichappiness.org, which is connected with Martin Seligman's book *Authentic Happiness*, which was written for the general public) that have online surveys on positive psychology. There are also a number of books that have exercises developed as a result of research in this field. Chief among these books are: Peterson's *A Primer in Positive Psychology*, Seligman's *Authentic Happiness*, and Boldt's *Pursuing Human Strengths*. Others are also listed in the selected bibliography on positive psychology provided in this book. If you are able to access some of these more general on-line surveys or exercises provided in the positive psychology books listed above and in the bibliography prior to responding to the more focused one below, it is preferable. If not, then the reader is urged to avail her/himself of them in the future since they have been developed by the current leaders in the field.

Below are questions designed specifically for clinicians. They have been formulated to stir up some initial reflection that is in line with some of the major themes of positive psychology as they relate to the clinicians themselves. A secondary goal is to interest clinicians to read further in the area from the books listed in the selected bibliography with an eye to deepening their own lives as well as to broadening the treatment approaches they take with their clients/patients.

The overarching aim of these goals is to encourage clinicians to enhance the paradigm for self-evaluation so that it is not just based on preventing, limiting, or ameliorating negative or unproductive habits, traits, or clinical styles. Given the training most psychologists, counselors, social workers, psychiatrists, psychiatric nurses, pastoral counselors, and other professional caregivers receive (e.g., awareness of one's countertransferences or recognizing an inability to provide accurate homework assignments to clients), this type of post-session reflection is usually a given. What is often absent, though, is a broader, more creative approach based on an appreciation of positive emotions and traits. As was noted, such thinking may not only improve client care but also temper the more negative critique undertaken so the self-awareness is more balanced, potent, and accurate. In the process, it can lead to a more creative, productive, and valid sense of one's overall professional and personal life as well. The result? A more healthy pursuit of human strengths and virtues, which, in turn, could lead to a more profound appreciation of what might contribute to a fuller life for both clinicians and their clients.

The clinician-client circle can then be gracefully completed by a clinician's broader positive sense of self because, once again, one of the greatest gifts we as clinicians can share with our clients is a sense of our own peace, joy, hope, and understanding of our strengths and virtues as well as what might block their development. However, we cannot share fully what we only have a partial awareness of; it is as simple as that.

Questions for Consideration

Who/what do you find are the persons and situations that
make life more joyful and meaningful for you?

How do you enhance these situations and nurture these relationships?

What do you consider to be your most important goals as a clinician and as a person?

How are you enjoying/flowing with the process to achieve this?

What are your major strengths and virtues?

How do you seek to apply them in daily life?

What are your particular talents as a clinician?

How do you foster their use—especially in enhancing your working alliance with clients?

What do you feel are the positive motivations for you to become and remain a clinician?

What are your strategies to face obstacles to your growth as a clinician and your style in encountering suffering/mortality that enables you to deepen and appreciate your life more fully—no matter what difficulties you may be facing?

What are some new clinical experiences that you were open to recently that you felt were broadening to you both as a clinician and a person?

What are some recent illustrations of how you were able to recognize your own emotions and creatively employ them in a clinical situation?

What are some of the approaches you use as a clinician to remove obstacles to your own growth?

In terms of your own strengths and virtues, what are illustrations of you at your best as a person? As a clinician?

How are these strengths and virtues connected with your overall philosophy as to what would make your life worth living?

How are you reinforcing these strengths and virtues?

What is the connection for you between exercising these strengths and (1) the development of rewarding relationships, (2) your sense of well-being as a person and clinician, and (3) your sense of psychological efficacy?

How has your own resiliency as a clinician been actually enhanced by very challenging client encounters?

In looking over your own life, what has made you value your life more deeply?

What are the ideas and beliefs you have about what makes you and others flourish as human beings?

What are some of the ways you ensure your autonomy as a clinician and person?

Given your career goals/personal mission in life, what is your specific plan to achieve it?

In what ways do you ensure your professional and personal life is balanced?

How would you describe your style of relating to those with whom you are most deeply connected?

What is it that clients and nonclients find most endearing about you?

What are some of the traits that you feel you have that you and others cherish? (Check each one that relates; after doing that, go back and double check ones that especially stand out for you.)

Dependable
Responsible
Open
Flexible
Welcoming

Trustworthy
Friendly
Hopeful
Understanding
Warm
Mature
Enjoyable to be with
Sympathetic
Encouraging
Energetic
A problem solver
A conflict resolver
Forgiving
Able to postpone gratification
Self-aware
Considers the greater good
Happy
Enthusiastic
Strong
Willing to listen
A life-long learner
Considerate
Romantic
Committed
Confident
Emotionally stable
Industrious
Sociable
Empathic
Able to form close relationships

Able to set aside time for reflection, silence, and
   solitude
Can easily share thoughts, feelings, and hopes with
   others
Can monitor and regulate one's own strong emotions
Deals well with ambiguities and surprises
Able to set priorities and follow them
Sees happiness, as opposed to pleasures, as important
   and knows what contributes to it
Sees mindfulness practices as valuable in one's own life
Has a balanced circle of friends
Able to laugh at myself
Optimistic

What are some interesting and unique ways you can use the
   above talents/gifts/strengths in your clinical practice and
   personal life?
What institutions (universities, health care facilities, religious/
   community/political organizations, professional associa-
   tions) are you involved in, and what are the benefits to you
   and the institution from these efforts on your part?
An article is written about you at the end of your life. What
   do you want included in it?
As you reflect on your life, for whom and what are you
   most grateful both professionally and personally? (Please
   be detailed.)
What are ways that you savor good experiences in your
   professional and personal life? (Provide illustrations.)
What are your favorite leisure activities?
How do you ensure they are present in your schedule?

How do you increase the frequency of contact with enjoyable, stimulating, encouraging, inspiring, humorous friends?

Given your knowledge of positive psychology, what are other questions you would ask yourself (as you would a client) that would open up a greater appreciation of the personal life you have and the meaningful work you do?

Clinician

An Honorable Profession, a Meaningful Life

I don't know what your destiny will be, but one thing
I do know, the only ones among you who will be
really happy are those who have sought and found
how to serve.

—Albert Schweitzer, humanitarian

Everyone needs resilience. More than fifty years of
scientific research have powerfully demonstrated that
resilience is the key to success at work and satisfaction in life. Where you fall on the resilience curve—
your natural reserves of resilience—affects your
performance in school and at work, your physical
health, your mental health, and the quality of your
relationships. It is the basic ingredient to happiness
and success.

—Karen Reivich and Andrew Shatté,
The Resilience Factor

Epilogue

In contemporary clinical practice, we focus so much on the challenges that we often fail to retain the balance that is achieved by also seeing what is so rewarding in the field and potentially renewing in our life in general. This is natural, as Vietnamese Zen Roshi Thich Nhat Hanh recognized when reflecting upon his helping role in a very dark time in his country and his own life:

> During the war, we were so busy helping the wounded that we sometimes forgot to smell the flowers. Night has a very pleasant smell [here], especially in the country. But we would forget to pay attention to the smell of mint, coriander, thyme, and sage. (1989, p. 16)

This book, then, has been about retaining an awareness of the rewards and deepening the gift of passion for the care of others while realistically facing the interior and systemic problems that are part of an involved life—especially in such personally and intellectually demanding fields as psychotherapy, counseling, and social work. It has also dealt with having an awareness of the acute and chronic dangers to one's health while not consequently forsaking the honor and privilege of working as a clinician. In addition, and of equal importance, it has also been about diagnosing the problems of secondary stress *early*, taking action—both preventive and ameliorative—as soon as possible and reviewing the results of such ongoing interventions. To do this, one has to be aware of what can be learned from the literature on the topic as well as from clinical work with people involved in mental health and social work today. But above all, it is about coming home to oneself in a way that self-knowledge, strengthening one's inner life, and self-care are not considered "a given" or "a luxury" but are instead intentionally embraced as part of an essential ongoing process of mindfulness. Such a process, like sound psychology, produces good results and a return to the wonder and awe that entering and remaining in the social work, counseling, and psychotherapy fields can and should produce.

There is a need for an ongoing monitoring of oneself and a continual posing of questions such as:

> What are the most helpful approaches I can take to deal with the systemic and personal stresses in my life?
> What additional knowledge/support do I need to take actions to accomplish a better program of self-care and increased self-knowledge?
> How can I strengthen my inner life through the use of mindfulness and positive psychology so I can have a richer personal and professional life?

In the previous four chapters, the many benefits of facing these questions in a conscious, ongoing (sometimes formal) way were enumerated. Accordingly, some of our primary goals should include:

- Having a sense of intrigue about our talents as well as our growing edges in a way to help deepen ourselves both as professionals and as persons;
- A recognition of the need for time apart to reflect, reassess, and replenish ourselves;
- Awareness of the signs of chronic irritability, fatigue, constant daydreaming, greater effort with less job satisfaction,

inability to relax, and a tendency to be preoccupied with work as warnings that chronic secondary stress needs to be limited before it becomes too severe;

- Appreciation of such signs of acute secondary stress (vicarious PTSD) as: persistent intrusive thoughts, distressing dreams and flashbacks while awake, an increased state of arousal and marked distrust of people and situations;
- Knowing the building blocks of mindfulness so both our professional and personal lives can become richer through meditation and daily practice of techniques that help us to be present, aware, and nonjudgmental in our observations; and
- Becoming appreciative of some of the key tenets of positive psychology so we can enhance not only the paradigm we use with our patients or clients but also how we view and approach ourselves as well.

THE JOYS OF CLINICAL WORK

In his foreword to an edited work by Schmuck and Sheldon (2001) on positive psychology, Csikszentmihalyi notes that

human beings are not just self-serving entities, but are rewarded also by a holistic principle of motivation. In other words, our well-being is enhanced when we devote energy to goals that go beyond the momentary and the selfish. We feel happier pursuing short-term goals than no goals at all; when pursing long-term goals rather than short-term ones;

when working to better ourselves rather than just having pleasure; and we feel happier when working for the well-being of another person, group, or larger entity as opposed to just investing effort in self-focused goals. These relationships seem to hold both at the momentary level of experience, and also developmentally, over the life-span—so that persons who devote more time to hierarchically more complex goals are also, on the whole, happier. (2001, p. 5)

Being a clinician offers us an opportunity to impact people's lives in so many obvious and subtle ways that are in line with what Csikszentmihalyi describes above as goals that produce happiness for the helper. These include:

- An opportunity to save or improve people's lives;
- Receiving trust and being part of the dramatic elements of peoples' lives not open to many other people/ professionals;
- Being part of a field whose knowledge base is dynamic and deep;
- Experiencing a sense of potency because of the impact we may have on other peoples' lives;
- Being given the opportunity to interact with a wide range of people and emotions in a myriad of situations;
- Being in a position to be both intrigued and challenged by the resistance of a problematic pattern (and sometimes the person carrying it!) to the treatment protocol we provide;
- Knowing firsthand the benefit of both good organization and creativity in providing sound treatment—and the

challenges that lie in knowing when one takes precedence over the other;
- Appreciating the essential role that our own personality, mindfulness, and overall psychological health have in delivering effective counseling, social work, and psychotherapy;
- Having the chance to be a "diagnostic detective" as we seek to uncover what symptoms and signs mean as we track and/or unmask a previously undiagnosed/undetected pattern in a patient.

The joys or job satisfaction can be so great. However, as in the case of self care, they are not a given. They must be appreciated and attended to in our lives. There is a need to raise our awareness of what the elements in job satisfaction are so we can turn the tide in favor of progress over the status quo. These may include: workload, variety, challenge, balance, positive feedback, mental stimulation, or an array of many factors that determine whether we wish to begin or continue in the helping professions.

In an article on caregiver satisfaction, similar sentiments are noted. One of the particular points made is that "higher perceived stress is associated with lower satisfaction levels that are related to greater intentions to quit, decrease work hours, change specialty, or leave direct patient care. One can see here the powerful effect of the combination of job stress and dissatisfaction. So powerful, in fact, that some of these highly trained, committed professionals may leave their practice situations while others cope by decreasing work hours, changing practice emphasis or leaving direct patient care" (Williams et al., 2001, p. 15).

When faced with stress, clinicians all act. The question *The Resilient Clinician* confronts is: *How do we act?* If we don't develop careful strategies, inactivity and unhealthy ones will certainly fill the void. It is my hope in writing this book that the reader will set aside the resistance that claims that approaches to understanding, limiting, and overcoming secondary stress are unrealistic or, worse, unnecessary. After reading this book, using the questionnaires as follow-up and revisiting this book when issues come up again—and they will—I believe that the practitioners will be able to navigate the waves of stress that are natural to clinical work in the most healthy and productive ways possible. Moreover, the result of such experiences will then position them to be open to be deeper persons and even more helpful as mentor to junior colleagues who, like them, continue to offer so much of themselves and deserve all the support and wisdom we can share with them.

Resilience is not something one can take for granted as a clinician. Maddi and Khoshaba in their book for a business audience, *Resilience at Work: How to Succeed No Matter What Life Throws at You*, note that

hardiness is a particular pattern of attitudes and skills that helps you to be resilient by surviving and thriving under stress. The attitudes are the 3Cs of commitment, control, and challenge. If you are strong in the 3Cs you believe that, as times get tough, it is best for you to stay involved with people and events around you (commitment) rather than to pull out, to keep trying to influence the outcomes in which you are involved (control) rather than to give up, and to try to discover how you and others can grow through stress (challenge) rather than to bemoan your fate. (2005, p. 13)

Following this approach, one of the steps that they suggest is to study people you know who are high in resilience. To do this, they pose the following five questions as a way of analyzing the approach this type of person has taken to transform stress into something advantageous for themselves:

1. *What stressful circumstances did he or she encounter?* Was the stress acute (disruptive and time limited) or chronic (a mismatch between dreams, desires, and actual experience)? Remember, sometimes an acute stress stirs up chronic stresses.

2. *What problem-solving actions did the person take to decrease the circumstances' stressfulness?* How did he or she do this? Did he or she follow up on opportunities stemming from the stressful situation?

3. *Did the person's coping efforts include getting supportive assistance and encouragement from other people?* Did he or she reach out to others as well in this process, and if so, how?

4. *How did this person talk about the experience?* When reminiscing, observing, planning, or evaluating the stress, did the person associate the experience with his or her life direction, purpose, and meaning? Did the evaluation express new insights about circumstance, life, and self?

5. *How did his or her coping efforts express hardy attitudes?* Can you fit what he or she said or did into commitment, control, and challenge (thought the problem was important and worthwhile enough to solve, tried to influence its outcome,

and used the experience to learn and grow from)?
(Maddi & Khoshaba, 2005, pp. 66, 67)

President John F. Kennedy used to tell the following story about one of his favorite authors:

Frank O'Connor, the Irish author, tells in one of his books how as a boy, he and his friends would make their way across the countryside and when they came to an orchard wall that seemed too high and too doubtful to try, and too difficult to permit their voyage to continue, they would take off their hats and toss them over the wall—and then they had no choice but to follow them! (Wicks, 1983)

As clinicians, in entering and continuing in the professions of counseling, psychotherapy, and social work, we have already thrown "our hats" over the wall. The information provided in this book is designed to offer some sense of direction with respect to secondary stress prevention, self-care, mindfulness, and the use of positive psychology in the self-debriefing so we can negotiate "the high walls" of clinical practice and remain firm in our commitment to our professions.

Causes of Burnout

1. Inadequate quiet time, . . . physical rest, cultural diversion, further education, and personal psychological replenishment.
2. Vague criteria for success and/or inadequate positive feedback on efforts made.
3. Guilt over failures and over taking out time to nurture oneself properly to deal with one's own legitimate needs.
4. Unrealistic ideals that are threatening rather than generally motivating.
5. Inability to deal with anger or other interpersonal tensions.
6. Extreme need to be liked by others, prompting unrealistic involvement with others.
7. Neglect of emotional, physical, and spiritual needs.
8. Poor community life and/or unrealistic expectations and needs surrounding the support and love of others for us. . . .
9. Working with people (peers, superiors, those coming for help) who are burned out.
10. Extreme powerlessness to effect needed change or being overwhelmed by paperwork and administrative tasks.

11. A serious lack of appreciation by our superiors, colleagues, or those whom we are trying to serve.
12. Sexism, ageism, racism, or other prejudice experienced directly in our lives and work.
13. High conflict in the family, home, work, or living environment.
14. A serious lack of charity among those with whom we must live or work.
15. Extreme change during times in life when maturational crises and adjustments are also occurring (for example, 48-year-old physician who is being asked to work with patients diagnosed with cancer at a time when she has just been diagnosed with cancer herself).
16. Seeing money wasted on projects that seem to have no relation to helping people or improving the health care system.
17. Not having the freedom or power to deal with or absent oneself from regularly occurring stressful events.
18. A failure to curb one's immature reasons for helping others and to develop more mature ones in the process.
19. The "savior complex"—an inability to recognize what we can and cannot do in helping others in need.
20. Overstimulation or isolation and alienation.

Level 1—Daily Burnout

A Sampling of Key Signs and Symptoms

Mentally fatigued at the end of the day

Feeling unappreciated, frustrated, bored, tense, or angry as a result of contact(s) with patients, colleagues, supervisors, superiors, assistants, or other potentially significant people

Experiencing physical symptoms (e.g., headache, backache, upset stomach, etc.)

Pace of day's activities and/or requirements of present tasks seem greater than personal or professional resources available

Tasks required on job are repetitious, beyond the ability of the [care giver], or require intensity on a continuous basis

Source: Wicks, R., Parsons, R., & Capps, D. (2003). *Clinical Handbook of Pastoral Counseling: Vol. 3*. Mahwah, NJ: Paulist Press. Used with permission.

Level 1—Daily Burnout

Steps for Dealing With Daily Burnout

1. Correcting one's cognitive errors so there is a greater recognition when we are exaggerating or personalizing situations in an inappropriate, negative way.
2. Having a variety of activities in one's daily schedule
3. Getting sufficient rest
4. Faithfully incorporating meditation [or quiet reflective time] in our daily schedule
5. Interacting on a regular basis with supportive friends
6. Being assertive
7. Getting proper nourishment and exercise
8. Being aware of the general principles set forth in the professional and self-help literature on stress management.

Source: Wicks, R., Parsons, R., & Capps, D. (2003). *Clinical Handbook of Pastoral Counseling: Vol. 3*. Mahwah, NJ: Paulist Press. Used with permission.

Level 2—Minor Stress Becomes Distress

Some Major Signs and Symptoms

Idealism and enthusiasm about being a [professional care giver] waning; disillusionment about [work] . . . surfacing on a regular basis

Experiencing a general loss of interest in the . . . field for a period of a month or longer

Pervasive feeling of boredom, stagnation, apathy, and frustration

Being ruled by schedule; seeing more and more patients; being no longer attuned to them; viewing them impersonally and without thought

Losing criteria with which to judge the effectiveness of work . . .

Inability to get refreshed by the other elements in one's life

A loss of interest in professional resources (e.g., books, conferences, innovations, etc.)

Intermittent lengthy (week or more) periods of irritation, depression, and stress that do not seem to lift even with some effort to correct the apparent causes

Source: Wicks, R., Parsons, R., & Capps, D. (2003). *Clinical Handbook of Pastoral Counseling: Vol. 3.* Mahwah, NJ: Paulist Press. Used with permission.

The Basics of Stress Management

PHYSICAL HEALTH

1. *Sleep*: Without enough sleep, the quality of what you do will decrease; rising early requires going to bed at a reasonable hour.
2. *Food*: Eating three light meals, at a reasonable pace, and being mindful of the nutritional value of what you eat is one of the best ways to keep weight down and nourishment and energy up.
3. *Exercise*: Taking a fairly brisk walk each day is a good minimum exercise. Doing it on a consistent basis is better than some irregular or future extensive exercise plan that we fail at and feel guilty about.
4. *Leisure*: Relaxing with your feet up and/or being involved in activities that provide genuine enjoyment are not niceties of physical health. Rather, they are undervalued but essential building blocks to good health. Leisure helps us "flow" with life's joys and problems in a more accepting philosophical way.

5. *Pacing*: Taking a little more time to get to a place makes the trip more relaxing; stopping every hour or hour and a half to get out of the car and stretch on long trips makes them a lot more enjoyable and helps increase stamina. Likewise, taking breaks when you feel the need makes your productivity better. The important lesson here is to use any technique necessary to slow yourself down so you don't rush to the grave missing the scenery in your life along the way.

PSYCHOLOGICAL STABILITY

1. *Laughter*: If laughter is good medicine, then surely laughing at yourself is healing. We all tend to take ourselves too seriously. So, doing something about this can significantly reduce unnecessary stress and help improve one's perspective on self and life.
2. *Values*: Know what is important and what isn't; by knowing what you believe to be really important, you can choose easily and well between alternatives.
3. *Control*: Be careful to discern between what you can control and what you can't; while worrying about something when it happens is natural, continuing to preoccupy yourself with it is not. When you catch yourself worrying endlessly, tease yourself that you must be "the world's best worrier." Then plan what you can do about it, and let it go. If and when it comes up again, review the process until it lessens or stops. This technique may need a good deal of practice for it to "take root" in your attitude.

4. *Self-Appreciation:* Reflect on what gifts . . . [have been] given you, recall them each day in detail (make a list if you have to on paper), and be grateful for them by promising to nurture and share them—not in a compulsive manner but in a generous way. By this I mean have low expectations that people will respond as you would wish or appreciate your efforts. However, simultaneously still try to maintain high hopes that you can appreciate . . . multiple measures of "success" in your work so you don't miss the good that is occurring before you because of a narrow success-oriented viewpoint. For instance, too often we measure what we achieve at the end of a process and fail to see or value appropriately all of the good we did along the way.

5. *Involvement, Not Over-Involvement:* Be active in what you feel is meaningful (the kind of things you would be pleased to reflect on at the very end of life—not necessarily those things that others might feel are impressive or important). Assertiveness on your part both to volunteer to be involved in what you believe is good and to say no to demands that aren't is also an essential part of increasing your involvement in stimulating activities and curbing (wherever possible) ones that are personally draining.

6. *Support Group:* Have people in your life who care; contact them frequently by phone and in writing as well as in person. Ideally, among this group should be a variety of psychologically healthy friends who can challenge, support, encourage, teach, and make you laugh.

7. *Escape:* There are times when we should "run away" because facing things directly in all of our relationships

all the time would be debilitating. To do this you can use novels, breaks during the day, movies, walks, hobbies (fishing, bicycle riding, etc.).

8. *Be Spontaneous:* A small creative action or change during the day or week can make life much more fun. This is a lot more practical than waiting for a yearly vacation.

9. *Be Careful of Negativity:* Often we hear negative comments like thunder and praise like a whisper. Use self-talk to catch your own negative tendencies (e.g., to see things in black-and-white terms, to exaggerate the negative, to let one negative event contaminate the whole day or week, or to discount other positive events). Then answer these thoughts with more accurate positive ones. For example, if you feel slightly depressed and check your thinking, you may see that because one thing went wrong today, you are saying to yourself that you are really a failure at what you do. By recognizing this exaggeration as nonsense, you can tell yourself more correctly that you made a mistake, not that you are a mistake! Following this, you can then recall successes you have had and bring to mind the faces of those who have been grateful for your presence in their lives. This will show you the face of [love] . . . in the world and help break the back of the strong, seamless negative thinking you are under at the time. Remember, negative thinking takes a good deal of energy. Stop it, and a great deal of energy will be freed up for growth and enjoyment.

10. *Check Your Individual Balance in the Areas of:*
    a. stimulation and quiet
    b. reflection and action
    c. work and leisure
    d. self-care and care of others
    e. self-improvement and patience
    f. future aspirations and present positive realities
    g. involvement and detachment.

Source: Wicks, Robert J. (1992). *Touching the Holy: Ordinariness, Self-Esteem and Friendship*. Notre Dame, IN: AMP. Used with permission.

Clinicians' Secondary Stress Self-Awareness Questionnaire

Permission to reprint this form can be gained without cost by indicating copyright (© 2008 Robert J. Wicks) and source (Wicks, R. [2008]. *The Resilient Clinician*. New York: Oxford University Press) and sending a written request indicating the reason and audience for its intended use to: Dr. Robert J. Wicks, Loyola College, 8890 McGaw Road, Suite 380, Columbia, MD 21045, USA, or via e-mail to rwicks@loyola.edu.

Instructions: Find a quiet, comfortable, and private place. Read each question and respond on a separate sheet of paper by writing the first thing that comes to mind. Once you have completed a page, do not turn back to it or refer to it when working on the other pages. Work as quickly as you can without setting a pace that is too stressful.

1. What is the reason you believe denial is so prevalent in the clinical setting with respect to stress for psychotherapists, social workers, and counselors? What are the most common lies you tell yourself about your own stress?

2. At this point, what are the most realistic and helpful steps you can take to prevent, limit, and learn from stress?

3. What are the ways you have heard that are excellent approaches to reducing stress and improving self-care but you feel are unrealistic in your case? What would it take to make them realistic? ("A miracle!" is not an acceptable answer.)

4. When you think of the terms "burnout," "compassion fatigue," and "chronic secondary stress," what do you think of in terms of your own life?

5. What are the issues that make you most anxious? What are the ones you deal with the best?

6. What are the types of situations or interactions from the past that still haunt you?

7. Given the realistic demands of work and family, what would it take to balance these two areas in your life a bit more? (List only those steps that can be realistically taken by you within the next two to three years.)

8. In your own case, what helps you to fall prey to the common masochistic tenet: The only worthy clinician is the one involved enough to be on the edge of burnout or physical fatigue?

9. In what ways did your professional schooling, clinical internship or field placements, modeling by supervisors, and initial work after graduation inadvertently teach you that taking care of yourself is a sign of weakness and an unhealthy life style is the price of being in the field of mental health/social work?

10. What are the "bad habits" of the people you observe in your profession that you don't want to emulate? How are you seeking to embrace the wonder, passion, and intense involvement in counseling, psychotherapy, or social work without also absorbing the pathological side of the profession?

11. When you are under a great deal of stress, what fantasies do you have? What do you think are healthy fantasies you should act upon some day? What are the unhealthy ones that, if acted upon, would cause you and others harm?

12. What elements that are in your self-care protocol now have been most beneficial for you? What are the least?

13. What do you struggle with most in your efforts to take care of yourself? Since your presence as a professional in the mental health or social work field means that de facto you are a bright and accomplished person, you wouldn't think these struggles should be so hard for you; why are they?

14. How would people describe your attitudes toward work?

15. What should be included in your list of personal doubts and insecurities that most people would be surprised to know about you?

16. In mental health, focus on the person and clinical situation that is before you is essential; what do you find are the main sources of external distraction and inner preoccupation that prevent you from doing this?

17. What are the most positive and negative impacts your personality style has on the way you interact with clients/patients? Staff?

18. When under extreme stress, what is the style of interacting with others and handling the situation that you would most like to change? What steps are necessary to produce such a change?

19. What would you include in your list of motivations for originally becoming a clinician? (Make the list as long as you can. Be sure to include any reasons you might now perceive as unrealistic or possibly immature—e.g., status, power over other people's life and death struggles, financial security, voyeurism, etc.—so you have as complete an accounting as possible.)

20. Have the primacy of certain motivations changed for you over time? If so, how? Why do you think this is so? If this is problematic in some way, what might you do about it? For those beneficial changes in priorities, how are you ensuring that they remain in focus for you?

21. What are the most awkward subjects for you to discuss in relationship to your emotional and physical well-being as a mental health or social work professional?

22. Where do you feel your narcissism comes into play in your role in health care?

23. What would be included in a list of what you like best about being a clinician? What would be on the list of what you like least?

24. What is most surprising to you about the professional life you now have?

25. What are the most frustrating aspects of your professional life? Your personal life?

26. If you have ever considered changing specialties or leaving the field, what are the reasons for this?

27. When you think of the profession you are now in, how would you describe it for someone thinking of entering the field now? Suppose someone asked you how you thought it would be different in five years; what would you say?

28. What are the most important self-care procedures you have put into place in the past five years? What has been their impact on you? In what ways would you now like to modify your plan?

29. Given your own personality style, what types of patients do you find most challenging? What types of colleagues, subordinates, and supervisors are able to easily elicit an emotional reaction from you? Given this, what ways have you found to most effectively interact with them? (Praying for their early, happy death is not a sufficient response.)

30. How would you describe the seemingly beneficial and adverse impact your professional life has had on your personal life and vice versa?

31. What are the five mistakes that you fear most in your work?

32. What stresses do you think you can lessen in your life by giving them some attention? What stresses do you feel powerless to alter?

33. How would you describe the differences in the sources of stress and the approaches to self-care between those for clinicians and those for other professions?

34. How self-aware do you feel you are? On what do you base this conclusion? What would help you gain greater self-awareness?

35. If you were to divide your personal needs for happiness into "necessary" and "desirable," what would be on each list? What would be on similar lists (necessary and desirable) for professional satisfaction and growth?

36. What information about yourself do you think you most like to hide even from yourself because it makes you uncomfortable to be aware of it?

37. What is your style of dealing with conflict? How would you improve your approach? To accomplish this, what is the next step you think you should take?

38. How much time alone do you need to remain balanced? What are the ways you see that such time is scheduled for yourself?

39. How do you know when you've lost your sense of perspective? What steps do you take to regain or maintain it?

40. What role does a sense of humor and laughter play in keeping yourself and the situation you are in from getting unnecessarily "heavy"?

41. What "little things" in life do you treasure and would you miss if they were not present in your life? What are the big things? How do you show that you appreciate them?

42. What professional accomplishments are you very proud of? What are some future ones you'd very much like to achieve?

43. Describe how you organize your schedule and how much control you have in your life. Are there ways this might be improved?

44. When and with whom are you most apt to react in an angry way? In a cowardly way? By withdrawing? Through avoidance?

45. Would you and others at work and home best describe you as assertive, passive, passive-aggressive, or aggressive? Is there a difference in your style between your personal and professional life? If so, how would you account for that?

46. What are the major areas of imbalance in your life? How are you addressing them? If you are not, what are some of the reasons you feel it is important to do so at this point in your life?

47. Do you know how to observe your feelings and behavior, then seek to see what cognitions (ways of thinking, perceiving, and understanding) and beliefs (schemata) are giving rise to them? If so, do you then dispute your dysfunctional thoughts as a way to keep perspective and avoid unnecessary stress/depressive thinking/self-condemnation? If not, how might you improve this area of self-awareness, self-monitoring, and increased recognition of the style of one's self-talk especially when under undue stress or after a failure?

48. What are the most unhealthy ways you are now meeting your needs or "medicating" yourself? What unhealthy gratifications are you concerned that you might avail

yourself of in the future? What are you doing to prevent, limit, or avoid this from happening?

49. What is the overall design of your daily, weekly, monthly, and yearly breaks for leisure, relaxation, quiet, and recreation? How would you describe your feelings about these times (e.g., guilt, "I deserve it," feeling uncomfortable, preoccupied with cases, blissful, resentment that they are too few and far between, etc.)?

50. What are the types of negative statements you normally make to yourself when you fail?

51. What are the healthiest ways you cope with life's difficulties? What are the most immature and unhealthy ways?

52. In what ways are you collaborative with other members of the health care team? What are the benefits and struggles you experience with such collaboration?

53. What professional and personal resentments do you still carry, and when are they most likely to surface?

54. Have you had any significant losses in the past several years? If so, what has your reaction been to them—initially, recently, now?

55. How do you view yourself in terms of physical aspects of your life (e.g., attractiveness, physical health, eating/drinking/weight/smoking/medication and illegal drug use, and exercise patterns)?

56. What is your reaction to the statement "Much of mental health care is still an art rather than an exact science"?

57. What are your feelings about asking for help in your personal life from your family? A colleague?

Professional organization? One's physician? A psychiatrist, psychologist, or counselor? A clergyperson?

58. In your professional life, when have you been tempted to step over personal, sexual, financial, or other appropriate boundaries you should have with your patients or colleagues?

59. Is there someone in your circle of friends who is both kind yet clear and direct with you so you would feel at ease to share anything but also would feel you are getting honest guidance?

60. In which clinical situations or with what type of clients do you feel most emotionally vulnerable? In other words, when have you reacted by going to either the extreme of overinvolvement or preoccupation or by closing down emotionally and seeing them as simply "a case" or "the borderline at 4:00 P.M."?

Individual Question Reflection Guide

1. We often tell ourselves lies about our behavior and make excuses for it because we don't want to give up the secondary gain involved or expend the effort needed to decrease the amount of stress we are under. Until the payoffs we receive for the behavior are unmasked as too costly and unnecessary, even the most destructive and immature defensive behavior will remain to cause us stress.

2. "Realistic" and "helpful" are important words in this question because they try to help us get around the resistance to change that is present when we feel any steps to reduce stress are beyond us; therefore, we don't have to do anything.

3. This question seeks to push us a bit farther in an effort to get us to be more assertive and creative in our planning and actions regarding the stress in life.

4. Too often we resist change by being global in our definitions of what's causing stress in our lives. This question seeks to get more specific causes out in the open so they can be addressed more directly either by ourselves or with our mentor or peer group.

5. This question allows us to make an inventory of our strengths and areas of vulnerability or growing edges. The longer and more detailed the two lists are, the more useful the responses will be. Also, looking for patterns in the list can be helpful in terms of planning interventions or attitude/schedule changes.

6. The only memory that is a problem is the one intentionally forgotten or unconsciously repressed because it retains power without our being aware of it. This question gives an opportunity to be honest again regarding those past events that are still sapping energy from us now and unconsciously impacting our behaviors in the present. PTSD includes such memories, but anyone who works in health care, by the nature of their work, has experienced traumatic occurrences and needs to have a clear awareness of them—not in order to blame oneself but to learn from them.

7. In the social work and mental health fields, there is a general tendency toward an imbalance in favor of work over one's personal life. This question provides an opportunity to take initial steps to change this imbalance a bit. One of the goals in phrasing the question again with the word "realistic" is to try to break the logjam that occurs when we feel overwhelmed and think nothing can be done. Perspective and attitude have tremendous power; whereas people who burnout often lose an awareness of this and feel unless someone else changes their environment, little of benefit can result.

8. Once we accept the mantle of "only a burned-out professional really cares and works hard," the psychological cost is immense. Moving against this societal and professional myth is essential if one is to undertake a program of self-care.

9. This is an opportunity to divide the people who we felt were professionally competent and personally attractive from the dysfunctional behavior they may have also modeled.

10. As a follow-up to question #9, this one asks for more information on how we can carry on the good heritage of our role models and leave their parallel defensive sides so we can become more healthy in how we carry out our work as clinicians.

11. There are some fantasies we should act on and others that would be dangerous if we did. Knowing the difference *ahead of time* is essential so that acting out or violating boundaries with colleagues or clients is never done with the rationalization after the fact that "It just happened."

12. This raises the need to have a self-care protocol and starts us to think in a more focused manner about the helpful and destructive ways one deals with the pressures in one's personal and professional life.

13. This question is designed to have one face their own resistances and defenses with the same energy and intellectual stamina as other issues one faces in life.

14. "Workaholism" is a pattern that seems to go unchecked in many a health care professional's life; this question

helps one not to gloss over the work style that everyone seems to acknowledge is present in us but we can't seem to fully grasp ourselves. People continue to endure an immense amount of unnecessary stress with either the response "It's part of the territory of being a clinician" or "That's just the way I am."

15. This allows us to take a step back and to acknowledge the human doubts and insecurities that all people have. This is important because much defensive or compensatory behavior is driven by such unexamined dynamics.

16. Distractions waste a tremendous amount of time in mental health and social work. Mistakes are often attributed to a lack of attention. This question helps us to see how we might systematically avoid unnecessary distraction or understand the dynamics involved in what needlessly preoccupies us at times when at work.

17. Making a list of how our personality both negatively and positively impacts certain types of individuals or all people when we are in certain moods equips us to better utilize our style of dealing with the world. By having greater awareness in this area, we can avoid so many potential relational problems that it is worth returning to this question to see what else we might add as illustrations of when and how we improved or made situations worse. It is very hard to do this because of the tendency to project the blame on a patient or staff member on the one hand or simply blame ourselves on the other. Clarity and a nonjudgmental approach to ourselves and our behavior are needed here.

18. Knowing your own stress points and when you are particularly vulnerable is essential. Even basic steps, such as knowing when to keep quiet until we understand why we are reacting so strongly and can regain more of our composure, can make a major difference in the stress level of interactions with others.

19. In many cases, we believe we know why we entered psychology, counseling, social work, psychiatric nursing, or other areas of mental health. However, there were many overlapping mature and immature reasons that we probably haven't thought about. Having this information is very valuable so that we can appreciate how to let the mature reasons grow and the other ones atrophy or take their proper place rather than ascending to a level where we make decisions for the wrong reasons.

20. Revisiting motivations that inspired and challenged us is essential if we are to keep and deepen the roles we have assumed in the lives of others. This reflection is very important especially with the jaded views of many in the culture with respect to health care and the possible beneficial roles they might play in it.

21. Many awkward subjects that are sensitive for us to discuss with others we don't really reflect on in safety with ourselves. This question gives us permission and encouragement to take out some time to look at what we are sensitive about and to start asking ourselves what we can do about it.

22. Healthy narcissism is good. It encourages us to take credit for good work, to be happy that we are in key

roles caring for others, and helps us recognize when we become defensive because our ego is getting in the way when it shouldn't.

23. This question reacquaints us with both the joy and pain of being a clinician. It is being asked so that there is greater clarity about what we don't like to see and how it can be changed in some way; even if we make minor alterations, when it is done in a number of areas this can provide great summative relief. But more than that, by getting clearer about what we like best, we can remember to enjoy and take strength from these areas when they are encountered each day.

24. This is a standard "taking stock" question that asks us what is going on that we didn't anticipate so that if we need to do something about it, we can do it before we get too derailed personally and professionally.

25. Frustrations drain energy. By naming them, we are taking the first step to understanding why they are so frustrating to us while others don't find them so. Once they can be understood in this way, they will lose some of their power; then we can catch ourselves when we repeat this pattern so we don't continue it any longer than need be.

26. Thoughts of job change often come during times when we have an aggregate of negative elements in our professional lives. By reviewing when and how we thought of moving or actually did, we can learn from this process in ways that prevent unnecessary moves or help us realize better when such a significant change is needed to relieve intractable stress or open up new possibilities.

27. This question is important for all of us to ask so we can be honest with ourselves as to how we feel about the field and our role in it. It also pulls us into the future to give some sense of the tone of our outlook and invites the question, What would I need to do to make this more positive for myself?

28. Our self-care protocol is examined here. At the very least, this question will encourage us to see if we have a plan in place. If it is informal, then it will help us write down what we are actually doing and give us a sense of how we might improve it.

29. Knowing who is able to "push our emotional buttons" is an important antidote to unnecessary stress. This question revisits this area so greater clarity, which is much needed on this topic if we are to remain psychologically healthy in tense situations, can be gained. Otherwise, the only thing that will happen is we will project the blame on certain types of people or blame ourselves for losing our temper or acting out.

30. Looking at the interchange between personal and professional well-being and how they impact each other helps us see that most adversity involves a more complex dynamic than we at first imagined it to have.

31. Breaking down fear into specifics allows us to discuss them with mentors and colleagues whom we trust so we can deal with the fears constructively rather than having them haunt us to no purpose. Just a naming and discussion of them can help alleviate stress in this area.

32. Powerlessness is an element in all of us. However, once again, perception and attention to such areas tend to diminish those areas that heretofore have been ignored and allowed to have control because of a lack of examination.

33. This is a chance to see what, if any, differences we feel about our profession and the stresses it holds as opposed to other fields. It allows us also to normalize some of our stress because we have much in common with many fields but don't often acknowledge this.

34. Methods to self-awareness such as reflection, meditation, journaling, receiving and giving supervision, personal daily debriefing, receiving mentoring, and formal/informal peer group discussions all can help us become better attuned to our styles. This question helps us visit this area to see if any or all of these approaches are present in some way and if not, why not.

35. By breaking down needs, we can begin to see those cases where we are depriving ourselves of essential needs for personal or professional well-being and where we have developed a series of induced needs that are psychologically costing us too much.

36. This question again visits the issue of shame. It allows us to free up those areas we have partially hidden even from ourselves so we can finally learn more from them and let them take a more appropriate place in our psyche rather than dominating it from within.

37. Each person has a different style of dealing with conflict. It is not good or bad, it just is. By taking this

approach and seeking to see the pros and cons of our style, we can take steps to improve upon it. Most people focus on whether the other person or they are right or wrong rather than on the style of conflict resolution. That is why this question if responded to in detail can produce much fruit and be a significant factor in stress reduction for ourselves and those with whom we interact.

38. Time alone is often considered a luxury or seems to just happen at times in our schedule. However, whether you are an introvert or an extrovert, time alone is psychologically needed for renewal, reflection, reassessment, and to break the movement of an often driven schedule. Having greater intention on where, how, and when to insert periods of solitude is necessary for one's mental health and, for those who are religiously minded, is an element of most major spiritualities.

39. Our loss of perspective is often more evident to others than to ourselves. However, there are signs that we have lost distance and a sense of proportion. They include: extreme emotion, withdrawal, an unnecessary increase in the pace of activity, or preoccupation. Once we know this, we can then ask ourselves how to best regain perspective. It may be by taking a few minutes alone on a short walk around the area in which our office/institution is located or to the lavatory, a phone call to a friend, or just remaining silent until we regain more of our composure. This approach helps us realize that each day we lose perspective and need to regain it in some way. It also prevents the three classic

dangers that come about when perspective is lost: projection, self-blame, and discouragement. Intrigue with
the dynamics within us as well as within the context
in which the loss of perspective occurred is naturally
more healthy and productive. Answering this question
fully helps support this good movement in our professional and personal lives.

40. Too often on the way to taking our work seriously,
    we take ourselves too seriously. This question high-
    lights this reality for all of us and helps us remember
    to continually appreciate that laughter is good medi-
    cine and a sense of humor keeps things light when-
    ever possible.

41. Deep gratefulness is one the major preventatives and
    antidotes to a loss of perspective. We have much to be
    grateful for—including our roles in health care, which
    not everyone can or is willing to undertake. Grateful-
    ness is not natural for most of us, whereas negative
    reactions seem to rise spontaneously and without effort.
    Self-training in this area starting with greater awareness
    that all is gift can provide an immeasurable factor in the
    prevention of burnout. This is so because when you are
    feeling constantly nourished by your surroundings, you
    retain a better sense of balance—gratefulness increases
    our sensitivity to what events and people are giving us
    so we don't take them for granted, belittle them, or in
    fact miss them.

42. Taking stock of your accomplishments is an act of
    healthy narcissism. It also aids, once again, in preven-
    tion of the loss of perspective that comes when we just

focus on the failures, absences, and struggles without seeing how far we have come. It also aids in planning for the future, which stirs up new hope in our hearts rather than having us just go through the motions every day.

43. Time management is often not taught in schools of counselor education, psychology, and social work. Yet, one of the causes of stress is disorganization or distraction at work. This question raises this issue to imply that there is more in our control than we are willing to acknowledge. In developing a self-care protocol, this area must be addressed in some way so we can use management/organizational skills to lessen stress. (This is addressed in chapter 2 on developing a self-care protocol, and further recommended readings in the area are included there as well.)

44. By picturing actual people in our lives who cause attack or flight reactions, we can begin to better understand what it is that this type of person is triggering in our lives so we can deal better with it. Once again, in most people's lives, the fact that certain people or personality types upset us is accepted as a given that can't be changed. In mental health and social work, this is a luxury of avoidance that must not be accepted because we need to deal with such persons again and again.

45. Appreciating our style by honestly looking at ourselves should be easier at this point in the questionnaire since by now, hopefully we are into the exercise of looking with a sense of intrigue and not with condemnation or denial. As we do this, it is important to begin to see the

differences in our styles at work and at home and try to better understand them. It will help in improving our interaction skills both at home and in the health care setting in which we work.

46. Imbalances need not remain in our lives. They also need not be radically corrected over night. Such a desire often ends up in our acting rashly rather than coura- geously to provide the necessary balance that will result in personal and professional well-being.

47. Picking up our feelings about things and then looking at what we are thinking and believing that may be dys- functional and responding to them with thoughts that are more healthy are important steps in maintaining perspective and mental health. This question highlights this and helps us to raise the volume of our "self-talk" so we don't let negative thinking act as the invisible puppeteer in our psyche.

48. Workaholism, alcohol abuse, improper use of medica- tion, sexual acting out, compulsive activity (eating, buying or gambling/stock market speculation) are but several ways we "medicate" ourselves. Knowing how, when, and to what extent we do this is an important first step to addressing this problematic area that is often one of the leading ones that we deny.

49. Time off during the day, week, month, and year is a conscious decision by those who effectively prevent and limit burnout. This area, as well as our feelings about it, is important to address as part of self-care.

50. Failure is part and parcel of involvement. The more we are involved and the more delicate problems we must

face in health care, the more we will fail. That is a statistical reality because we can't be perfect. Case closed. Therefore, knowing how we deal with failure, since it is often a part of what we do, would help diminish unnecessary anxiety and avoidable stress.

51. This question addresses overall style when we are faced with obstacles and asks for an inventory of our talents and defenses. As in some of the other questions, this seeks a review and also goes hand in hand with other questions to check the reliability of our previous responses.

52. Collaboration has often been seen as necessary but not realistic by many in health care. Yet, health care, to be effective, needs to be a team effort in which each member of the team is respected, given as much autonomy as is appropriate, and has input into the health care program offered for the patient. An individual's understanding and attitude toward collaboration is explored in this question.

53. Resentments are psychological powder kegs that lie in the preconscious and may break through when triggered by an event or person in our environment— especially when sleep deprivation or another problem or lack is present to make us more vulnerable. Unearthing these resentments so they don't remain as hidden psychological cancers, which go unnoticed but continue to grow and devour us from within, is obviously necessary.

54. Since dealing with the issues of death and dying is part of the territory for health care professionals, being

aware of our own losses and how we have dealt with or avoided dealing with them is quite helpful.

55. Taking note of our physical prowess and those elements that add or are destructive to it is something that is paradoxically avoided by many in health care. This question asks for a detailed response that is undertaken without blame but with honesty and a willingness to consider measured change that won't be abandoned, as in the case of a diet that leaves us permanently deprived.

56. Not every error in mental health and social work is malpractice. No clinician can be perfect in their diagnosis or intervention with all clients or patients. This is a reality of the fact that clinical work itself is not perfect. How we answer this question provides some insight into our view of the expectations we have of ourselves and the field.

57. We can never go it alone. Also, sometimes it is important to treat ourselves to a defined period of therapy or mentoring so we can work through failures, deepen our personal lives, and learn new creative ways of improving personal and professional well-being. This question looks at how we avail ourselves of help, collaboration, supervision, and support.

58. Honesty in this question allows us to pick up the "emotional flags" that will warn us when we might violate boundaries with a patient or colleague. Everyone has a vulnerable place in their lives where boundary violation is possible. Knowing ahead of time what this may be or

what type of person we would be most vulnerable with is essential.

59. This asks the question, with whom do we feel both freedom and clarity? At the very least, asking it points to the tenet that if we don't have a person like this, we run the risk of going off course in our professional and personal lives. It also points to the need to ensure we have steady contact with someone like this, and if we don't, to find someone who can fit this role.

60. Becoming callous or overemotional is a constant danger in being a clinician. This question is designed to help us explore when and how this happens. As in the other questions in this questionnaire, it is asking us not to take our reactions for granted but to explore them further so we can both understand ourselves better and plan for change that is productive both professionally and personally.

Works Cited

"An interview with Thich Nhat Hanh, Vietnamese Zen Master," *Common Boundary*, Nov./Dec. 1989, p. 16.

Auden, W. H. (1976). Introduction. In D. Hammarskjold (Ed.), *Markings* (p. ix). New York: Knopf.

Baker, E. (2003). *Caring for ourselves: A therapist's guide to personal and professional well-being.* Washington, DC: American Psychological Association.

Bloom, A. (1970). *Beginning to pray.* Ramsey, NJ: Paulist Press.

Bode, R. (1993). *First you have to row a little boat.* New York: Warner.

Brazier, D. (1954/1995). *Zen therapy.* New York: Wiley.

Buber, M. (1966). *Way of man.* New York: Lyle Stuart.

Buchholz, E. (1997). *The call of solitude: Alonetime in a world of attachment.* New York: Simon & Schuster.

Burns, D. (1980). *Feeling good.* New York: New American Library.

Byrd, R. (1938/1995). *Alone.* New York: Kodansha.

Chadwick, D. (1999). *The crooked cucumber.* New York: Broadway.

Chodron, P. (1997). *When things fall apart.* Boston: Shambala.

Coster, J., & Schwebel, M. (1997). Well-functioning in professional psychologists. *Professional Psychology: Research and Practice, 28,* 10.

Works Cited

Courtois, C. A. (1999). *Recollections of sexual abuse: Treatment principles and guidelines.* New York: W. W. Norton & Co.

Cozolino, L. (2004). *The making of a therapist: A practical guide for the inner journey.* New York: W. W. Norton & Co.

Csikszentmihalyi, M. (2000). *Beyond boredom and anxiety.* San Francisco: Jossey-Bass. (Original work published in 1975).

Dalai Lama. (2000). *The path to tranquility.* New York: Penguin.

Domar, A., & Dreher, H. (2000). *Self-nurture: Learning to care for yourself as effectively as you care for everyone else.* New York: Penguin.

Dubois, D. (1983). Renewal of prayer. *Lumen Vitae, 38*(3), 273–274.

Edelwich, J., & Brodsky, A. (1980). *Burnout.* New York: Human Sciences Press.

Foy, D., Drescher, K., Fits, A., & Kennedy, K. (2003). Post-traumatic stress disorders. In R. Wicks, R. Parsons, & D. Capps (Eds.), *Clinical handbook of pastoral counseling: Vol. 3* (pp. 274–277). Mahwah, NJ: Paulist Press.

Fredrickson, B. L. (1998). What good are positive emotions? *Review of General Psychology, 2,* 300–319.

Fredrickson, B. L. (2000). Cultivating positive emotions to optimize health and well-being. *Prevention and Treatment, 3.* Document available at http://journals.apa.org/prevention. Accessed February 8, 2005.

Fredrickson, B. L. (2001). The role of positive emotions in positive psychology: The broaden-and-build theory of positive emotions. *American Psychologist, 56,* 218–226.

Fredrickson, B. L. (2004). The broaden-and-build theory of positive emotions. *Philosophical Transactions of the Royal Society of London (Biological Sciences), 359,* 1367–1377.

Germer, C. K., Siegel, R. D., & Fulton, P. R. (Eds.). (2005). *Mindfulness and psychotherapy.* New York: Guilford Press.

Gill, J. (1980). Burnout: A growing threat in ministry. *Human Development, 1,* 24–25.

Gorky, M. (1996). *Gorky: My childhood.* London: Penguin.

Gunaratana, B. (2002). *Mindfulness in plain English.* Somerville, MA: Wisdom Publications.

Hay, G. (1967). *The way to happiness.* New York: Simon & Schuster.

Herman, J. (1997). *Trauma and recovery: The aftermath of violence—from domestic abuse to political terror.* New York: Basic Books.

Kabat-Zinn, J. (1994). *Wherever you go, there you are: Mindfulness meditation in everyday life.* New York: Hyperion.

Kaplan, A. (1982). *Meditation and Kabbalah.* York Beach, ME: Samuel Weiser.

Keller, P. A., & Ritt, L. (Eds.). (1984). *Innovations in clinical practice: A sourcebook: Vol. 3.* Sarasota, FL: Professional Resource Exchange.

Kornfield, J. (1993). *A path with heart: A guide through the perils and promises of spiritual life.* New York: Bantam.

Kornfield, J. (2000). *After the ecstasy, the laundry: How the heart grows wise on the spiritual path.* New York: Bantam.

Kottler, J. (1989). *On being a therapist.* San Francisco: Jossey-Bass.

Kottler, J. A., & Hazler, R. J. (1997). *What you never learned in graduate school: A survival guide for therapists.* New York: W. W. Norton & Co.

Leech, K. (1980). *True prayer.* San Francisco: Harper & Row.

Linehan, M. (1993). *Cognitive-behavioral treatment of borderline personality disorder.* New York: Guilford Press.

Linehan, M. (2005). This one moment: Skills for everyday mindfulness [DVD]. Behavioral Tech, LLC, Seattle, WA.

Lynn, K. S. (1987). Ernest Hemingway: A psychological autopsy of a suicide. *Psychiatry: Interpersonal & Biological Processes, 69,* 351–361.

Maddi, S. R., & Khoshaba, D. M. (2005). *Resilience at work: How to succeed no matter what life throws at you.* New York: American Management Association.

Maslach, C., & Jackson, S. E. (1981). The measurement of experienced burnout. *Journal of Occupational Behavior, 2,* 99–113.

McCaffrey , R., & Fairbank, J. (1985). Behavioral assessment and treatment of accident-related posttraumatic stress disorder: Two case studies. *Behavior Therapy, 16,* 406–416.

Merton, T. (1988). *A vow of conversation.* New York: Farrar, Straus, & Giroux.

Morgan, S. (2005). Depression: Turning toward life. In C. K. Germer, R. D. Siegel, & P. R. Fulton (Eds.), *Mindfulness and psychotherapy* (pp. 130–151). New York: Guilford Press.

Nouwen, H. (1981). *Making all things new.* New York: Harper & Row.

Parsons, R. D., & Wicks, R. J. (Eds). (1983). *Passive-aggressiveness: Theory and practice.* New York: Brunner/Mazel.

Peterson, C. (2006). *A primer in positive psychology.* New York: Oxford University Press.

Pfifferling, J. H. (1986). Cultural antecedents promoting professional impairment. In C. D. Scott & J. Hawk (Eds.), *Heal thyself: The health of health care professionals* (pp. 3–18). New York: Brunner/Mazel.

Pope, K. S., & Vasquez, M. J. T. (2005). *How to survive and thrive as a therapist.* Washington, DC: American Psychological Association.

Reinhold, B. B. (1997). *Toxic work: How to overcome stress, overload and burnout and revitalize your career.* New York : Plume.

Reivich, K., & Shatté, A. (2002). *The resilience factor: 7 keys to finding your inner strength and overcoming life's hurdles.* New York: Broadway Books.

Riegle, R. (2003). *Dorothy Day: Portraits by those who knew her.* Maryknoll, NY: Orbis.

Rilke, R. M. (1954/2004). *Letters to a young poet* (Rev. ed.). New York: W. W. Norton & Co.

Rinpoche, S. (1992). *The Tibetan book of living and dying.* New York: Harper Collins.

Rodman, R. (1985). *Keeping hope alive.* New York: Harper & Row.

Sanders, L. (1982). *The case of Lucy Bending.* New York: Putnam.

Schmuck, P., & Sheldon, K. M. (2001). Introduction. In P. Schmuck & K. M. Sheldon (Eds). *Life goals and well-being: Towards a positive psychology of human striving.* Cambridge, MA: Hogrefe & Huber Publishing.

Scott, C., & Hawk, J. (Eds.). (1986). *Health thyself: The health of health care professionals.* New York: Brunner/Mazel.

Seaward, B. (2000). *Managing stress in emergency medical services.* Sudbury, MA: American Academy of Orthopaedic Surgeons/Jones & Bartlett.

Seligman, M. E. P. (2002). *Authentic happiness: Using the new positive psychology to realize your potential for lasting fulfillment.* New York: Free Press.

Skovolt, T. M. (2001). *The resilient practicioner: Burnout prevention and self-care strategies for counselors, therapists, teachers, and health professionals.* Boston: Allyn & Bacon.

Storr, A. (1988). *On solitude.* New York: Bantam.

Strand, C. (1988). *The wooden bowl.* New York: Hyperion.

Sussman, M. B. (1992). *A curious calling: Unconscious motivations for practicing psychotherapy.* Northvale, NJ: Jason Aronson.

Warner, C. (1992). *The last word: A treasury of women's quotes.* Englewood Cliffs, NJ: Prentice Hall Trade.

Weiss, A. (2004). *Beginning mindfulness: Learning the way of awareness.* Novato, CA: New World Library.

Wicks, R. (1986). *Availability.* New York: Crossroad.

Wicks, R. (1988). *Living simply in an anxious world.* Mahwah, NJ: Paulist Press.

Wicks, R. (1992). *Touching the holy.* Notre Dame: Ave Maria Press.

Wicks, R. (1995). The stress of spiritual ministry: Practical suggestions on avoiding unnecessary distress. In R. Wicks (Ed.), *Handbook of spirituality for ministers: Vol. 1,* pp. 249–258. Mahwah, NJ: Paulist Press.

Wicks, R. (1997). *After 50: Spiritually embracing your own wisdom years.* New York: Paulist Press.

Wicks, R. (1998). *Living a gentle, passionate life.* Mahwah, NJ: Paulist Press.

Wicks, R. (2000). *Simple changes.* Notre Dame: Thomas More/Sorin Books.

Wicks, R. (2002). *Riding the dragon.* Notre Dame: Sorin Books.

Works Cited

Wicks, R. (2003). Countertransference and burnout in pastoral counseling. In R. Wicks, R. Parsons, & D. Capps (Eds.), *Clinical handbook of pastoral counseling: Vol. 3*, pp. 321–341. Mahwah, NJ: Paulist Press.

Wicks, R. (2006). *Overcoming secondary stress in medical and nursing practice: A guide to professional resilience and personal well-being.* New York: Oxford University Press.

Wicks, R., & Hamma, R. (1996). *Circle of friends: Encountering the caring voices in your life.* Notre Dame: Ave Maria Press.

Williams, E., Konrad, T., Scheckler, W., Pathman, D., Linzer, M., McMurray, J., et al. (2001). Understanding physicians' intentions to withdraw from practice: The role of job satisfaction, job stress, and mental and physical health. *Health Care Management Review, 26*, 7–19.

Zaslove, M. (2001). American Academy of Family Physicians. *Curbside consultation: A case of physician burnout.* American Family Physician. Available at http://www.aafp.org/afp/2001/08/01/curbside.html.

Selected Bibliography

The following lists contain only book-length treatments of the topic. This is done so that if additional reading is desired, the sources can be quickly obtained. The last section (General Sources) also contains articles and papers.

Clinician Self-Care, Secondary Stress, and Resiliency

Baker, E. K. (2002). *Caring for ourselves: A therapist's guide to personal and professional well-being.* Washington, DC: American Psychological Association.

Domar, A. D., & Dreher, H. (2001). *Self-nurture: Learning to care for yourself as effectively as you care for everyone else.* New York: Penguin.

Kottler, J. A. (2003). *On being a therapist.* San Francisco: John Wiley & Sons.

Leiter, M. P., & Maslach, C. (2005). *Banishing burnout: Six strategies for improving your relationship with work* (3rd ed.). San Francisco: Jossey-Bass.

Pope, K. S., & Vasques, M. J. T. (2005). *How to survive and thrive as a therapist.* Washington, DC: American Psychological Association.

Reinhold, B. B. (1997). *Toxic work: How to overcome stress, overload and burnout and revitalize your career.* New York: Plume.

Reivich, K., & Shatté, A. (2002). *The resilience factor: 7 keys to finding your inner strength and overcoming life's hurdles.* New York: Broadway Books.

Rothschild, B., & Rand, M. (2006). *Help for the helper: The psychophysiology of compassion fatigue and vicarious trauma.* New York: W. W. Norton & Co.

Skovholt, T. M. (2001). *The resilient practitioner: Burnout prevention and self-care strategies for counselors, therapists, teachers, and health professionals.* Boston: Allyn & Bacon.

Weiss, L. (2004). *Therapist's guide to self-care.* New York: Routledge/Taylor & Francis.

Mindfulness

Batchelor, S. (1997). *Buddhism without beliefs.* New York: Riverhead Books.

Beck, C. (1989). *Everyday Zen: Love and work.* San Francisco: Harper San Francisco.

Brach, T. (2003). *Radical acceptance: Embracing your life with the heart of a Buddha.* New York: Bantam Dell.

Brantley, J. (2003). *Calming your anxious mind.* Oakland, CA: New Harbinger Publications.

Brazier, D. (1995). *Zen therapy.* New York: John Wiley.

Chodron, P. (2001). *The wisdom of no escape and the path of loving-kindness.* Boston: Shambhala Publications.

Dalai Lama & Cutler, H. (1998). *The art of happiness: A handbook for living.* New York: Riverhead.

Epstein, M. (1995). *Thoughts without a thinker: Psychotherapy from a Buddhist perspective.* New York: Basic Books.

Germer, C., Siegel, R., & Fulton, P. (Eds.) (2005). *Mindfulness and psychotherapy.* New York: Guilford Press.

Selected Bibliography

Goldman, D. (2003). *Destructive emotions: How can we overcome them?* New York: Bantam Dell.

Goldstein, J. (1993). *Insight meditation: The practice of freedom.* Boston: Shambhala Publications.

Goldstein, J., & Kornfield, J. (1987). *Seeking the heart of wisdom.* Boston: Shambhala Publications.

Gunaratana, D. (2002). *Mindfulness in plain English.* Somerville, MA: Wisdom Publications.

Hanh, T. N. (1975/1987). *The miracle of mindfulness.* Boston: Beacon Press.

Hayes, S., Follette, V., & Linehan, M. (Eds.) (2004). *Mindfulness and acceptance: Expanding the cognitive-behavioral tradition.* New York: Guilford Press.

Kabat-Zinn, J. (1990). *Full catastrophe living.* New York: Delacorte Press.

Kabat-Zinn, J. (1994). *Wherever you go, there you are: Mindfulness meditation in everyday life.* New York: Hyperion.

Kabat-Zinn, J. (2005a). *Coming to our senses: Healing ourselves and the world through mindfulness.* New York: Hyperion.

Kabat-Zinn, J. (2005b). *Guided mindfulness meditation.* (Series 1–3 [Compact disc]). Box 547, Lexington, MA: Stress Reduction CDs and Tapes.

Kabat-Zinn, M., & Kabat-Zinn, J. (1998). *Everyday blessings: The inner work of mindful parenting.* New York: Hyperion.

Kornfield, J. (1993). *A path with heart: A guide through the perils and promises of spiritual life.* New York: Bantam.

Kornfield, J. (2000). *After the ecstasy, the laundry: How the heart grows wise on the spiritual path.* New York: Bantam.

Langer, E. (1989). *Mindfulness.* Cambridge, MA: Da Capo Press.

Linehan, M. (2005) *This one moment: Skills for everyday mindfulness.* Seattle: Behavioral Tech.

Salzberg, S. (1995). *Loving kindness: The revolutionary art of happiness.* Boston: Shambhala Publications.

Stern, D. (2004). *The present moment in psychotherapy and everyday life.* New York: W. W. Norton & Co.

Suzuki, S. (1973). *Zen mind, beginner's mind.* New York: John Weatherhill.

Weiss, A. (2004). *Beginning mindfulness: Learning the way of awareness.* Novato, CA: New World Library.

Wicks, R. (2003). *Riding the dragon.* Notre Dame: Soren Books.

Positive Psychology

Aspinwall, L. G., & Staudinger, U. M. (Eds.). (2003). *A psychology of human strengths: Fundamental questions and future directions for a positive psychology.* Washington, DC: American Psychological Association.

Baumeister, R. F. (2005). *The cultural animal: Human nature, meaning, and social life.* Oxford: Oxford University Press.

Csikszentmihalyi, M. (1990). *Flow: The psychology of optimal experience.* New York: Harper Perenniel.

Csikszentmihalyi, M. (1998). *Finding flow: The psychology of engagement with everyday life.* New York: Basic Books.

Csikszentmihalyi, M., & Csikszentmihalyi, I. S. (Eds.) (2006). *A life worth living: Contributions to positive psychology.* New York: Oxford University Press.

Emmons, R. A., & McCullough, M. E. (Eds.). (2004). *The psychology of gratitude.* Oxford: Oxford University Press.

Fowers, B. J. (2005). *Virtue and psychology: Pursuing excellence in ordinary practices.* Washington, DC: American Psychological Association.

Gilbert, D. (2006). *Stumbling on happiness.* New York: Alfred A. Knopf.

Haidt, J. (2006). *The happiness hypothesis: Finding modern truth in ancient wisdom.* New York: Basic Books.

James, W. (2002). *The varieties of religious experience: A study in human nature.* New York: Modern Library.

Keyes, C. L. M., & Haidt, J. (2002). *Flourishing: Positive psychology and the life well-lived.* Washington, DC: American Psychological Association.

Linley, P. A., & Joseph, A. (Eds.) (2004). *Positive psychology in practice.* Hoboken, NJ: John Wiley & Sons.

Maslow, A. H. (1968/1999) (3rd ed.). *Toward a psychology of being.* New York: John Wiley & Sons.

Norem, J. K. (2001). *The positive power of negative thinking.* Cambridge, MA: Basic Books.

Pearsall, P. (2003). *The Beethoven factor: The new positive psychology of hardiness, happiness, healing, and hope.* Charlottesville, VA: Hampton Roads Publishing Co.

Peterson, C. (2006). *A primer in positive psychology.* New York: Oxford University Press.

Peterson, C., & Seligman, M. E. P. (Eds.). (2004). *Character strengths and virtues: A handbook and classification.* Oxford: American Psychological Association & Oxford University Press.

Seligman, M. E. P. (1990/1998). *Learned optimism: How to change your mind and your life.* New York: Pocket Books

Seligman, M. E. P. (1993). *What you can change...and what you can't: The complete guide to successful self-improvement.* New York: Ballantine Books.

Seligman, M. E. P. (2002). *Authentic happiness: Using the new positive psychology to realize your potential for lasting fulfillment.* New York: Free Press.

Snyder, C. R., & Lopez, S. J. (Eds.). (2002). *Handbook of positive psychology.* Oxford: Oxford University Press.

General Sources

Ackerley, G. D., Burnell, J., Holder, D. C., & Durdek, L. A. (1988). Burnout among licensed psychologists. *Professional Psychology: Research and Practice, 19,* 624–631.

Adams, R. E., Boscarino, J. A., & Figley, C. R. (2006). Compassion fatigue and psychological distress among social workers: A validation study. *American Journal of Orthopsychiatry, 76,* 103–108.

Adler, G. (1972). Helplessness in the helpers. *British Journal of Medical Psychology, 45,* 315–326.

Alloy, L. B., & Abramson, L. Y. (1982). Learned helplessness, depression, and the illusion of control. *Journal of Personality and Social Psychology, 36*, 1114–1126.

Ammerman, R. T., Cassisi, J. E., Hersen, M., & Van-Hasselt, V. B. (1986). Consequences of physical abuse and neglect in children. *Clinical Psychology Review, 6*, 291–310.

"An interview with Thich Nhat Hanh, Vietnamese Zen Master," *Common Boundary*, Nov./Dec. 1989, p. 16.

Aragones, A. (2001). Burnout among doctoral level psychologists: A study of coping alternatives (Doctoral dissertation, University of Detroit Mercy, 1999). *Dissertation Abstracts International, 61*, 3886.

Arnold, D., Calhoun, L. G., Tedeschi, R., & Cann, A. (2005). Vicarious posttraumatic growth in psychotherapy. *Journal of Humanistic Psychology, 45*, 239–263.

Aspinwall, L. G., & Staudinger, U. M. (Eds.). (2003). *A psychology of human strengths: Fundamental questions and future directions for a positive psychology.* Washington, DC: American Psychological Association.

Auden, W. H. (1976). Introduction. In D. Hammarskjold (Ed.), *Markings* (p. ix). New York: Knopf.

Baker, E. (2003). *Caring for ourselves: A therapist's guide to personal and professional well-being.* Washington, DC: American Psychological Association.

Barnett, J., & Sarnel, D. (n.d.). *No time for self-care?* Retrieved June 30, 2006, from http://www.division42.org/StEC/articles/transition/no_time.html.

Barnes, R. C. (1994). Finding meaning in unavoidable suffering. *International Forum for Logotherapy, 17*, 20–26.

Batchelor, S. (1997). *Buddhism without beliefs.* New York: Riverhead Books.

Baumeister, R. F. (2005). *The cultural animal: Human nature, meaning, and social life.* Oxford: Oxford University Press.

Beck, C. (1989). *Everyday Zen: Love and work.* San Francisco: Harper San Francisco.

Becvar, D. S. (2003). The impact on the family therapist of a focus on death, dying, and bereavement. *Journal of Marital and Family Therapy, 29*, 469–477.

Bell, H., Kulkarni, S., & Dalton, L. (2003). Organizational prevention of vicarious trauma. *Families in Society: The Journal of Contemporary Human Services, 84*, 463–470.

Bloom, A. (1970). *Beginning to pray.* Ramsey, NJ: Paulist.

Bode, R. (1993). *First you have to row a little boat.* New York: Warner.

Bodnar, J. C., & Kiecolt-Glaser, J. K. (1994). Caregiver depression after bereavement: Chronic stress isn't over when it's over. *Psychology and Aging, 9*(3), 372–380.

Bolt, M. (2004). *Pursuing human strengths: A positive psychology guide.* New York: Worth Publishers.

Bowers, B. J. (2005). *Virtue and psychology: Pursuing excellence in ordinary practices.* Washington, DC: American Psychological Association.

Brach, T. (2003). *Radical acceptance: Embracing your life with the heart of a Buddha.* New York: Bantam Dell.

Brantley, J. (2003). *Calming your anxious mind.* Oakland, CA: New Harbinger Publications.

Brazier, D. (1995). *Zen therapy.* New York: John Wiley.

Briere, J. (1989). *Therapy for adults molested as children: Beyond survival.* New York: Springer.

Brooks, Jr., C. W. (2000). The relationship among substance abuse counselors' spiritual well-being, values, and self-actualizing characteristics and the impact on clients' well-being. *Journal of Addictions & Offender Counseling, 21*(1), 23–33.

Brown, III, F. M. (2002). Inside every chronic patient is an acute patient wondering what happened. *JCLP/In Session: Psychotherapy in Practice, 58*, 1443–1449.

Buber, M. (1966). *Way of man.* New York: Lyle Stuart.

Buchholz, E. S. (1997). *The call of solitude: Alonetime in a world of attachment.* New York: Simon & Schuster.

Burns, D. (1980). *Feeling good.* New York: New American Library.

Butollo, W. H., & Ludwig-Maximillians, U. (1996). Psychotherapy integration for war traumatization: A training project in central Bosnia. *European Psychologist, 1,* 140–146.

Byrd, R. (1938/1995). *Alone.* New York: Kodansha.

Caldwell, M. P. (1984). Stress/distress/burnout: A perspective for counseling and therapy. *Individual Psychology: Journal of Adlerian Theory, Research & Practice, 40,* 475–483.

Capner, M., & Caltabiano, M. L. (1993). Factors affecting the progression towards burnout: A comparison of professional and volunteer counsellors. *Psychological Reports, 73,* 555–561.

Case, P. W., & McMinn, M. R. (2001). Spiritual coping and well-functioning among psychologists. *Journal of Psychology and Theology, 29,* 29–40.

Chadwick, D. (1999). *The crooked cucumber.* New York: Broadway.

Cherniss, C. (1980). *Staff burnout: Job stress in the human services.* Newbury Park, CA: Sage Publications.

Chodron, P. (1997). *When things fall apart.* Boston: Shambhala.

Chodron, P. (2001). *The wisdom of no escape and the path of loving-kindness.* Boston: Shambhala Publications.

Cohen, M., & Gagin, R. (2005). Can skill-development training alleviate burnout in hospital social workers? *Social Work in Health Care, 40,* 83–97.

Collins, S. (2003). Working with the psychological effects of trauma: Consequences for mental health-care workers: A literature review. *Journal of Psychiatric and Mental Health Nursing, 10,* 417–424.

Collins, W. L. (2005). Embracing spirituality as an element of professional self-care. *Social Work & Christianity, 32,* 263–274.

Coons, C. M. (2001). Student's corner: Avoiding premature exasperation: 10 habits of highly successful counselors. *Annals of the American Psychotherapy Association, 4*(5), 25.

Coster, J. S., & Schwebel, M. (1997). Well-functioning in professional psychologists. *Professional Psychology: Research and Practice, 28,* 5–13.

Courtois, C. A. (1988). *Healing the incest wound: Adult survivors in therapy.* New York: W. W. Norton & Co.

Courtois, C. A. (1999). *Recollections of sexual abuse: Treatment principles and guidelines.* New York: W. W. Norton & Co.

Coyle, D., Edwards, D., Hannigan, B., Fothergill, A., & Burnard, P. (2005). A systematic review of stress among mental health social workers. *International Social Work, 48,* 201–211.

Cozolino, L. (2004). *The making of a therapist: A practical guide for the inner journey.* New York: W. W. Norton & Co.

Csikszentmihalyi, M. (1990). *Flow: The psychology of optimal experience.* New York: Harper Perenniel.

Csikszentmihalyi, M. (1998). *Finding flow: The psychology of engagement with everyday life.* New York: Basic Books.

Csikszentmihalyi, M. (2000). *Beyond boredom and anxiety.* San Francisco: Jossey-Bass. (Original work published in 1975).

Cunningham, M. (1999). The impact of sexual abuse treatment on the social work clinician. *Child and Adolescent Social Work Journal, 16,* 277–290.

Cunningham, M. (2003). Impact of trauma work on social work clinicians: Empirical findings. *Social Work, 48,* 451–459.

Cunningham, M. (2004). Teaching social workers about trauma: Reducing the risks of vicarious traumatization in the classroom. *Journal of Social Work Education, 40,* 305–317.

Cushway, D. (1996). Tolerance begins at home: Implications for counsellor training. *International Journal for the Advancement of Counselling, 18,* 189–197.

Cushway, D., & Tyler, P. (1996). Stress in clinical psychologists. *International Journal of Social Psychiatry, 42,* 141–149.

Dalai Lama. (2000). *The path to tranquility.* New York: Penguin.

Dalai Lama, & Cutler, H. (1998). *The art of happiness: A handbook for living.* New York: Riverhead.

Dane, B., & Chachkes, E. (2001). The cost of caring for patients with an illness: Contagion to the social worker. *Social Work in Health Care, 33,* 31–51.

Davis, D. C., & Markley, B. L. (2000). College counselors' well being. In D. C. Davis & K. M. Humphrey (Eds.), *College counseling: Issues and strategies for a new millennium* (pp. 267–287). Alexandria, VA: American Counseling Association.

Davis, S. (August 2003). Can caregivers care too much? *DVM Newsmagazine,* 58–59. Retrieved August 29, 2006, from www.dvmnewsmagazine.com.

Dienstbier, R. A. (1989). Arousal and physiological toughness: Implications for mental and physical health. *Psychological Review, 96,* 84–100.

Domar, A. D., & Dreher, H. (2000). *Self-nurture: Learning to care for yourself as effectively as you care for everyone else.* New York: Penguin.

Dubois, D. (1983). Renewal of prayer. *Lumen Vitae, 38*(3), 273–274.

Edelwich, J., & Brodsky, A. (1980). *Burnout.* New York: Human Sciences Press.

Edward, K. (2005). The phenomenon of resilience in crisis care mental health clinicians. *International Journal of Mental Health Nursing, 14,* 142–148.

Edwards, R. (1995). "Compassion fatigue": When listening hurts. *Monitor on Psychology, 26*(5), 34.

Egan, M. (1993). Resilience at the front lines: Hospital social work with AIDS patients and burnout. *Social Work in Health Care, 18,* 109–125.

Emmons, R. A., & McCullough, M. E. (Eds.). (2004). *The psychology of gratitude.* Oxford: Oxford University Press.

Ensman, Jr., R. G. (2000). Are you a burnout candidate? *Case Manager, 11,* 59–61.

Epstein, M. (1995). *Thoughts without a thinker: Psychotherapy from a Buddhist perspective.* New York: Basic Books.

Etherington, K. (2000). Supervising counsellors who work with survivors of childhood sexual abuse. *Counselling Psychology Quarterly, 13,* 377–389.

Evans, T. D., & Villavisanis, R. (1997). Encouragement exchange: Avoiding therapist burnout. *Family Journal: Counseling and Therapy for Couples and Families, 5,* 342–345.

Figley, C. R. (Ed.) (1995). *Compassion fatigue: Coping with secondary trau-matic stress disorder in those who treat the traumatized.* London: Routledge.

Figley, C. R. (2002). Compassion fatigue: Psychotherapists' chronic lack of self-care. *Journal of Clinical Psychology, 58*(11), 1433–1441.

Florian, V., Mikulincer, M., & Taubman, O. (1995). Does hardiness con-tribute to mental health during a stressful real-life situation? The roles of appraisal and coping. *Journal of Personality and Social Psychology, 68,* 687–695.

Foa, E. B., Steketee, G., & Rothbam, B. O. (1989). Behavioral/cognitive conceptualizations of post-traumatic stress. *Journal of Traumatic Stress, 1,* 291–304.

Fowers, B. J. (2005). *Virtue and psychology: Pursuing excellence in ordinary practices.* Washington, DC: American Psychological Association.

Fox, R. (2003). Traumaphobia: Confronting personal and professional anxiety. *Psychoanalytic Social Work, 10,* 43–55.

Fox, R., & Carey, L. A. (1999). Therapists' collusion with the resistance of rape survivors. *Clinical Social Work Journal, 27*(2), 185–201.

Fox, R., & Cooper, M. (26). The effects of suicide on the private practi-tioner: A professional and personal perspective. *Clinical Social Work Journal, 26,* 143–157.

Foy, D., Drescher, K., Fits, A., & Kennedy, K. (2003). Post-traumatic stress disorders. In R. Wicks, R. Parsons, & D. Capps (Eds.), *Clinical handbook of pastoral counseling: Vol. 3* (pp. 274–277). Mahwah, NJ: Paulist Press.

Foy, D. W., Osato, S., Houskamp, B., & Neumann, D. (1991). Etiology factors in posttraumatic stress disorder. In P. Saigh (Ed.), *Posttrau-matic stress disorder: A behavioral approach to assessment and treatment* (pp. 28–49). Oxford: Pergamon Press.

Foy, D. W., Siprelle, R. C., Rueger, D. B., & Carroll, E. M. (1984). Etiology of posttraaumatic stress disorder in Vietnam veterans: Analysis of pre-military, military, and combat exposure influences. *Journal of Consult-ing and Clinical Psychology, 52,* 79–87.

Fredrickson, B. L. (1998). What good are positive emotions? *Review of General Psychology, 2*, 300–319.

Fredrickson, B. L. (2000). Cultivating positive emotions to optimize health and well-being. *Prevention and Treatment, 3.* Document available at http://journals.apa.org/prevention. Accessed February 8, 2005.

Fredrickson, B. L. (2001). The role of positive emotions in positive psychology: The broaden-and-build theory of positive emotions. *American Psychologist, 56*, 218–226.

Fredrickson, B. L. (2004). The broaden-and-build theory of positive emotions. *Philosophical Transactions of the Royal Society of London (Biological Sciences), 359*, 1367–1377.

Freudenberger, H. J., & North, G. (1985). *Women's burnout: How to spot it, how to reverse it and how to prevent it.* Garden City, NY: Doubleday & Co., Inc.

Ganster, D. C. (1987). Type A behavior and job stress. In J. M. Ivanevich & D. C. Ganster (Eds.), *Job stress: From theory to suggestion.* New York: Haworth Press.

Garfinkel, P. E., & Waring, E. M. (1981). Personality, interests, and emotional disturbance in psychiatric residents. *American Journal of Psychiatry, 138*, 541–551.

Garmezy, N., & Masten, A. S. (1986). Stress, competence, and resilience: Common frontiers for therapist and psychopathologist. *Behavioral Therapy, 17*, 500–521.

Geller, J. A., Madsen, L. H., & Ohrenstein, L. (2004). Secondary trauma: A team approach. *Clinical Social Work Journal, 32*, 415–430.

Germer, C. K., Siegel, R. D., & Fulton, P. R. (Eds.) (2005). *Mindfulness and psychotherapy.* New York: Guilford Press.

Gilbert, D. (2006). *Stumbling on happiness.* New York: Alfred A. Knopf.

Gill, J. (1980). Burnout: A growing threat in ministry. *Human Development, 1*, 21–25.

Glickauf-Hughes, C., & Mehlman, E. (1995). Narcissistic issues in therapists: Diagnostic and treatment considerations. *Psychotherapy, 32*, 213–221.

Goldman, D. (2003). *Destructive emotions: How can we overcome them?* New York: Bantam Dell.

Goldstein, J. (1993). *Insight meditation: The practice of freedom.* Boston: Shambhala Publications.

Goldstein, J., & Kornfield, J. (1987). *Seeking the heart of wisdom.* Boston: Shambhala Publications.

Gorky, M. (1996). *Gorky: My childhood.* London: Penguin.

Grafanaki, S., Pearson, D., Cini, F., Godula, D., McKenzie, B., Nason, S., et al. (2005). Sources of renewal: A qualitative study on the experience and role of leisure in the life of counsellors and psychologists. *Counselling Psychology Quarterly, 18,* 31–40.

Green, B. L., Grace, M. C., & Gleser, G. C. (1985). Long-term impairment following the Beverly Hills Supper Club fire. *Journal of Consulting & Clinical Psychology, 53,* 672–678.

Groves, J. E. (1978). Taking care of the hateful patient. *New England Journal of Medicine, 298*(16), 883–887.

Gunaratana, B. (2002). *Mindfulness in plain English.* Somerville, MA: Wisdom Publications.

Haidt, J. (2006). *The happiness hypothesis: Finding modern truth in ancient wisdom.* New York: Basic Books.

Hanh, T. N. (1975/1987). *The miracle of mindfulness.* Boston: Beacon Press.

Hay, G. (1967). *The way to happiness.* New York: Simon & Schuster.

Hayes, S., Follette, V., & Linehan, M. (Eds.). (2004). *Mindfulness and acceptance: Expanding the cognitive-behavioral tradition.* New York: Guilford Press.

Herman, J. (1997). *Trauma and recovery: The aftermath of violence—from domestic abuse to political terror.* New York: Basic Books.

Hesse, A. R. (2002). Secondary trauma: How working with trauma survivors affects therapists. *Clinical Social Work Journal, 30*(3), 293–309.

Holmqvist, R., & Andersen, K. (2003). Therapists' reactions to treatment of survivors of political torture. *Professional Psychology: Research and Practice, 34*(3), 294–300.

Horwitz, M. (1998). Social worker trauma: Building resilience in child protection social workers. *Smith College Studies in Social Work, 68*, 363–377.

Houskamp, B. (1991). The assessment of PTSD in battered women. *Journal of Interpersonal Violence, 6*(3), 367–375.

Huggard, P. (2003). Compassion fatigue: How much can I give? *Medical Education, 37*, 163–164.

Huxley, P., Evans, S., Gately, C., Webber, M., Mears, A., Pajak, S., et al. (2005). Stress and pressures in mental health social work: The worker speaks. *British Journal of Social Work, 35*, 1063–1079.

Inbar, J., & Ganor, M. (2003). Trauma and compassion fatigue: Helping the helpers. *Journal of Jewish Communal Service, 79*, 109–111.

Jackson, S. (1983). Participation in decision making as a strategy for reducing job-related strain. *Journal of Applied Psychology, 68*, 3–19.

Jackson, S., & Maslach, C. (1982). After-effects of job-related stress: Families as victims. *Journal of Occupational Behavior, 3*, 63–77.

Jackson, S., & Schuler, R. (1985). A meta-analysis and conceptual critique of research on role conflict in work settings. *Organizational Behavior and Human Decision Processes, 36*, 16–78.

Jackson, S., Schwab, R., & Schuler, R. (1986). Toward an understanding of the burnout phenomenon. *Journal of Applied Psychology, 71*, 630–640.

Jaffe, D. T. (1986). The inner strains of healing work: Therapy and self-renewal for health professionals. In C. D. Scott & J. Hawk (Eds.), *Heal thyself: The health of health care professionals* (pp. 134–146). New York: Brunner/Mazel.

James, W. (2002). *The varieties of religious experience: A study in human nature.* New York: Modern Library.

Jenkins, S. R., & Baird, S. (2002). Secondary traumatic stress and vicarious trauma: A validational study. *Journal of Traumatic Stress, 15*, 423–432.

Jones, S. H. (2005). A self-care plan for hospice workers. *American Journal of Hospice & Palliative Medicine, 22*, 125–128.

Justice, B., Gold, R., & Klein, J. (1981). Life events and burnout. *Journal of Psychology, 108*, 219–226.

Kabat-Zinn, J. (1990). *Full catastrophe living*. New York: Delacorte Press.

Kabat-Zinn, J. (1994). *Wherever you go, there you are: Mindfulness meditation in everyday life*. New York: Hyperion.

Kabat-Zinn, J. (2005). *Coming to our senses: Healing ourselves and the world through mindfulness*. New York: Hyperion.

Kabat-Zinn, J. (2005). *Guided mindfulness meditation. Series 1–3*. (Compact disc). Box 547, Lexington, MA: Stress Reduction CDs and Tapes.

Kabat-Zinn, M., & Kabat-Zinn, J. (1998). *Everyday blessings: The inner work of mindful parenting*. New York: Hyperion.

Kahn, W. J. (1976). Self-management: Learning to be our own counselor. *Personnel and Guidance Journal, 55*, 176–180.

Kaplan, A. (1982). *Meditation and Kabbalah*. York Beach, ME: Samuel Weiser.

Keane, T. M., Fairbank, J. A., Caddell, J. M., & Zimering, R. T. (1989). Therapy reduces symptoms of PTSD in Vietnam combat veterans. *Behavior Therapy, 20*, 245–260.

Keller, P. A., & Ritt, L. (Eds.). (1984). *Innovations in clinical practice: A sourcebook: Vol. 3*. Sarasota, FL: Professional Resource Exchange.

Kennedy, N. (2004). Connected separateness or separate connection: Envisioning body with mind. *Journal of Health Care for the Poor and Underserved, 15*, 501–505.

Kesler, K. D. (1990). Burnout: A multimodal approach to assessment and resolution. *Elementary School Guidance & Counseling, 24*(4), 303–312.

Keyes, C. L. M., & Haidt, J. (2002). *Flourishing: Positive psychology and the life well-lived*. Washington, DC: American Psychological Association.

Kleespies, P. M., & Dettmer, E. L. (2000). The stress of patient emergencies for the clinician: Incidence, impact, and means of coping. *Journal of Clinical Psychology, 58*, 1353–1369.

Koeske, G. F., & Koeske, R. D. (1989). Work load and burnout: Can social support and perceived accomplishment help? *Social Work, 34,* 243–248.

Kolb, L. C. (1988). A critical survey of hypotheses regarding posttraumatic stress disorders in light of recent research findings. *Journal of Traumatic Stress, 1,* 291–304.

Kornfield, J. (1993). *A path with heart: A guide through the perils and promises of spiritual life.* New York: Bantam.

Kornfield, J. (2000). *After the ecstasy, the laundry: How the heart grows wise on the spiritual path.* New York: Bantam.

Kottler, J. A. (1989). *On being a therapist.* San Francisco: John Wiley & Sons.

Kottler, J. A. (2001). *The therapist's workbook: Self-assessment, self-care, and self-improvement exercises for mental health professionals.* San Francisco: John Wiley & Sons.

Kottler, J. A., & Hazler, R. J. (1997). *What you never learned in graduate school: A survival guide for therapists.* New York: W. W. Norton & Co.

Kraus, V. I. (2005). Relationship between self-care and compassion satisfaction, compassion fatigue, and burnout among mental health professionals working with adolescent sex offenders. *Counseling and Clinical Psychology Journal, 2,* 81–88.

Kumar, S., Hatcher, S., & Huggard, P. (2005). Burnout in psychiatrists: An etiological model. *International Journal of Psychiatry in Medicine, 35,* 405–416.

Kuyken, W., Peters, E., Power, M. J., & Lavender, T. (2003). Trainee clinical psychologists' adaptation and professional functioning: A longitudinal study. *Clinical Psychology and Psychotherapy, 10,* 1041–1054.

Langer, E. (1989). *Mindfulness.* Cambridge, MA: Da Capo Press.

Lazarus, R. S. (1966). *Psychological stress and the coping process.* New York: McGraw-Hill.

Lee, R. T., & Ashforth, B. E. (1990). On the meaning of Maslach's three dimensions of burnout. *Journal of Applied Psychology, 75*(6), 743–747.

Leech, K. (1980). *True prayer.* San Francisco: Harper & Row.

Leighton, S. L., & Roye, A. K. (1984). Prevention and self-care for professional burnout. *Family & Community Health, 6*, 44–56.

Leiter, M. P. (1990). Coping patterns as predictors of burnout: The function of control and escapist coping patterns. *Journal of Organzational Behavior, 11*, 123–144.

Leiter, M. P., & Maslach, C. (1988). The impact of interpersonal environment on burnout and organizational committment. *Journal of Organizational Behavior, 9*, 297–308.

Leiter, M. P., & Maslach, C. (2005). *Banishing burnout: Six strategies for improving relationship with work* (3rd ed.). San Francisco: Jossey-Bass.

Lepnurm, R., Dobson, R., Backman, A., & Keegan, D. (2006). Factors explaining career satisfaction among psychiatrists and surgeons in Canada. *Canadian Journal of Psychiatry, 51*, 243–255.

Linehan, M. (1993). *Cognitive behavioral treatment of borderline personality disorder.* New York: Guilford Press.

Linehan, M. M., Cochran, B. N., Mar, C. M., Levensky, E. R., & Comtios, K. A. (2000). Therapeutic burnout among borderline personality disordered clients and their therapists: Development and evaluation of two adaptations of the Maslach Burnout Inventory. *Cognitive and Behavioral Practice, 7*, 329–337.

Linehan, M. (2005). This one moment: Skills for everyday mindfulness [DVD].

Linley, P. A., & Joseph, A. (Eds.). (2004). *Positive psychology in practice.* Hoboken, NJ: John Wiley & Sons.

Lynn, K. S. (1987). Ernest Hemingway: A psychological autopsy of a suicide. *Psychiatry: Interpersonal & Biological Processes, 69*, 351–361.

Maddi, S. R. (2002). The story of hardiness: Twenty years of theorizing, research, and practice. *Consulting Psychology Journal: Practice and Research, 54*, 175–185.

Maddi, S. R., & Hightower, M. (1999). Hardiness and optimism as expressed in coping patterns. *Consulting Psychology Journal: Practice and Research, 51*, 95–105.

Maddi, S. R., & Khoshaba, D. M. (2005). *Resilience at work: How to succeed no matter what life throws at you.* New York: American Management Association.

Martin, Jr., W. E., Easton, C., Wilson, S., Takemoto, M., & Sullivan, S. (2004). Salience of emotional intelligence as a core characteristic of being a counselor. *Counselor Education & Supervision, 44,* 17–30.

Maslach, C., & Goldberg, J. (1998). Prevention of burnout: New perspectives. *Applied & Preventive Psychology, 7,* 63–74.

Maslach, C., & Jackson, S. E. (1981). The measurement of experienced burnout. *Journal of Occupational Behavior, 2,* 99–113.

Maslow, A. H. (1968/1999). *Toward a psychology of being* (3rd ed.). New York: John Wiley & Sons.

Matthews, D. B. (1990). A comparison of burnout in selected occupational fields. *The Career Development Quarterly, 38,* 230–239.

Mazza, N. (1997). Beyond burnout: Helping teachers, nurses, therapists, and lawyers recover from stress and disillusionment/secondary traumatic stress: Self-care issues for clinicians, researchers, and educators. *Health & Social Work, 22,* 77.

McCaffrey, R., & Fairbank, J. (1985). Behavioral assessment and treatment of accident-related posttraumatic stress disorder: Two case studies. *Behavior Therapy, 16,* 406–416.

McDermott, D. (1984). Professional burnout and its relation to job characteristics, satisfaction, and control. *Journal of Human Stress, 10,* 79–85.

McMillan, I. (2006, February). Practitioners warned of the emotional burden of caring. *Mental Health Practice, 9,* 34.

Medeiros, M. E., & Prochaska, J. O. (1988). Coping strategies that psychotherapists use in working with stressful clients. *Professional Psychology: Research and Practice, 19*(1), 112–114.

Merton, T. (1988). *A vow of conversation.* New York: Farrar, Straus, & Giroux.

Miller, L. (1998). Our own medicine: Traumatized psychotherapists and the stresses of doing therapy. *Psychotherapy: Theory, Research, Practice, Training, 35*(2), 137–146.

Morgan, S. (2005). *Depression: Turning toward life.* In C. K. Germer, R. D. Siegel, & P. R. Fulton (Eds.), *Mindfulness and psychotherapy* (pp. 130–151). New York: Guilford Press.

Morgan, L. D., & Hellkamp, D. T. (1991). Burnout among consulting psychologists in Division 13 of APA. *Consulting Psychology Bulletin, 42,* 1–6.

Morgan, W. D., & Morgan, S. T. (2005). Cultivating attention and empathy. In C. K. Germer, R. D. Siegel, & P. R. Fulton (Eds.), *Mindfulness and psychotherapy* (pp. 73–83). New York: Guilford.

Muscroft, J., & Hicks, C. (1998). A comparison of psychiatric nurses' and general nurses' reported stress and counseling needs: A case study approach. *Journal of Advanced Nursing, 27,* 1317–1326.

Nelson-Gardell, D., & Harris, D. (2003). Childhood abuse history, secondary traumatic stress, and child welfare workers. *Child Welfare, 82,* 5–26.

Norem, J. K. (2001). *The positive power of negative thinking.* Cambridge, MA: Basic Books.

Nouwen, H. (1981). *Making all things new.* New York: Harper & Row.

O'Halloran, T. M., & Linton, J. M. (2000). Stress on the job: Self-care resources for counselors. *Journal of Mental Health Counseling, 22*(4), 354–365.

Osborn, C. J. (2004). Seven salutary suggestions for counselor stamina. *Journal of Counseling and Development, 82,* 319–328.

Pardess, E. (2005). Training and mobilizing volunters for emergency response and long-term support. *Journal of Aggression, Maltreatment & Trauma, 10,* 609–620.

Parsons, R. D., & Wicks, R. J. (Eds). (1983). *Passive-aggressiveness: Theory and practice.* New York: Brunner/Mazel.

Patrick, P. K. (1987). Hospice caregiving: Strategies to avoid burnout and maintain self-preservation. *Hospice Journal, 3,* 223–253.

Pearsall, P. (2003). *The Beethoven factor: The new positive psychology of hardiness, happiness, healing, and hope.* Charlottesville, VA: Hampton Roads Publishing Co.

Peterson, C. (2006). *A primer in positive psychology.* New York: Oxford University Press.

Peterson, C., & Seligman, M. E. P. (Eds.). (2004). *Character strengths and virtues: A handbook and classification.* Oxford: American Psychological Association & Oxford University Press.

Pfifferling, J. H. (1986). Cultural antecedents promoting professional impairment. In C. D. Scott & J. Hawk (Eds.), *Heal thyself: The health of health care professionals* (pp. 3–18). New York: Brunner/Mazel.

Pfifferling, J. H., & Gilley, K. (2000). Overcoming compassion fatigue: When practicing medicine feels more like labor than a labor of love, take steps to heal the healer. *Family Practice Management, 7,* 39–45.

Pieper, M. H. (1999). The privilege of being a therapist: A fresh perspective from intrapsychic humanism on caregiving intimacy and the development of the professional self. *Families in Society, 80*(5), 479–487.

Pines, A. M. (1986). Who is to blame for helpers' burnout? Environmental impact. In C. D. Scott & J. Hawk (Eds.), *Heal thyself: The health of health care professionals* (pp. 19–43). New York: Brunner/Mazel.

Pines, A. M., Aronson, E., & Kafry, D. (1981). *Burnout: From tedium to personal growth.* New York: Free Press.

Pines, A., & Maslach, C. (1978). Characteristics of staff burn-out in mental health settings. *Hospital and Community Psychiatry, 29,* 233–237.

Pockett, R. (2003). Staying in hospital social work. *Social Work in Health Care, 26,* 1–24.

Pope, K. S., & Tabachnick, B. G. (1993). Therapists' anger, hate, fear, and sexual feelings: National survey of therapist responses, client characteristics, critical events, formal complaints, and training. *Professional Psychology: Research and Practice, 24,* 142–152.

Pope, K. S., & Tabachnick, B. G. (1994). Therapists as patients: A national survey of psychologists' experiences, problems, and beliefs. *Professional Psychology: Research and Practice, 25,* 247–258.

Pope, K. S., Tabachnick, B. G., & Keith-Spiegel, P. (1987). Ethics of practice: The beliefs and behaviors of psychologists as therapists. *American Psychologist, 42,* 993–1006.

Pope, K. S., & Vasquez, M. J. T. (2005). *How to survive and thrive as a therapist.* Washington, DC: American Psychological Association.

Puchalski, C. M. (2001). Spirituality and health: The art of compassionate medicine. *Hospital Physician, 37,* 30–36.

Ramirez, A. J., Graham, J., & Richards, M. A., et al. (1995). Burnout and psychiatric disorder among cancer clinicians. *Breast Cancer Journal, 71,* 1263–1269.

Ramirez, A. J., Graham, J., & Richards, M. A., et al. (1996). Mental health of hospital consultants: Effects of stress and satisfaction at work. *Lancet, 347,* 724–728.

Raquepaw, J. M., & Miller, R. W. (1989). Psychotherapist burnout: A componential analysis. *Professional Psychology: Research and Practice, 20(1),* 32–36.

Rasmussen, B. (2005). An intersubjective perspective on vicarious trauma and its impact on the clinical process. *Journal of Social Work Practice, 19,* 19–30.

Reid, Y., Johnson, S., Morant, N., Kuipers, E., Szmukler, G., Thornicroft, G., et al. (1999). Explanations for stress and satisfaction in mental health professionals: A qualitative study. *Social Psychiatry and Psychiatric Epidemiology, 34,* 301–308.

Reinhold, B. B. (1997). *Toxic work: How to overcome stress, overload and burnout and revitalize your career.* New York : Plume.

Reivich, K., & Shatte, A. (2002). *The resilience factor: 7 keys to finding your inner strength and overcoming life's hurdles.* New York: Broadway Books.

Riegle, R. (2003). *Dorothy Day: Portraits by those who knew her.* Maryknoll, NY: Orbis.

Rilke, R. M. (1954/2004). *Letters to a young poet* (Rev. ed.). New York: W. W. Norton & Co.

Rinpoche, S. (1992). *The Tibetan book of living and dying.* New York: Harper Collins.

Riordan, R. J., & Saltzer, S. K. (1992). Burnout prevention among health care providers working with the terminally ill: A literature review. *Omega, 25,* 17–24.

Rodman, R. (1985). *Keeping hope alive.* New York: Harper & Row.

Rothschild, B., & Rand, M. (2006). *Help for the helper: The psychophysiology of compassion fatigue and vicarious trauma.* New York: W. W. Norton & Co.

Rowe, M. M. (1997). Hardiness, stress, temperament, coping, and burnout in health professionals. *American Journal of Health Behavior, 21,* 163–172.

Rupert, P. A., & Baird, K. A. (2004). Managed care and the independent practice of psychology. *Professional Psychology: Research and Practice, 35,* 185–193.

Russell, A. T., Pasnau, R. O., & Taintor, Z. C. (1975). Emotional problems of residents in psychiatry. *American Journal of Psychiatry, 132,* 263–267.

Rybak, C. J., Leary, A., & Marui, A. (2001). The resiliency wheel: A training model for enhancing the effectiveness of cross-cultural interviews. *International Journal for the Advancement of Counselling, 23,* 7–19.

Sabin-Farrell, R., & Turpin, G. (2003). Vicarious traumatization: Implications for the mental health of health workers? *Clinical Psychology Review, 23,* 449–480.

Salmon, P. (2001). Effects of physical exercise on anxiety, depression, and sensitivity to stress: A unifying theory. *Clinical Psychology Review, 21,* 33–61.

Salston, M. D., & Figley, C. R. (2003). Secondary traumatic stress effects of working with survivors of criminal victimization. *Journal of Traumatic Stress, 16,* 167–174.

Salzberg, S. (1995). *Loving kindness: The revolutionary art of happiness.* Boston: Shambhala Publications.

Sanders, L. (1982). *The case of Lucy Bending.* New York: Putnam.

Sarata, B. P. (1983). Burnout workshops for alcoholism counselors. *Journal of Alcohol and Drug Education, 28*(3), 34–46.

Schauben, L. J., & Frazier, P. A. (1995). Vicarious Trauma: The effects on female counselors of working with sexual violence survivors. *Psychology of Women Quarterly, 19,* 49–64.

Schaufelli, W. B., Maslach, C., & Marek, T. (Eds.). (1993). *Professional burnout: Recent developments in theory and research.* New York: Taylor & Francis.

Schmuck, P., & Sheldon, K. M. (2001). Introduction. In P. Schmuck & K. M. Sheldon (Eds.), *Life goals and well-being: Towards a positive psychology of human striving.* Cambridge, MA: Hogrefe & Huber Publishing.

Schoen, K. (1998). Caring for ourselves: Understanding and minimizing the stresses of HIV caregiving. In D. Aronstein & B. Thompson (Eds.), *HIV and social work: A practitioner's guide* (pp. 527–559). New York: Hawthorne Press.

Scott, C. D., & Hawk, J. (Eds.). (1986). *Heal thyself: The health of health care professionals.* New York: Brunner/Mazel.

Seaward, B. (2000). *Managing stress in emergency medical services.* Sudbury, MA: American Academy of Orthopaedic Surgeons/Jones & Bartlett.

Seligman, M. E. P. (1990/1998). *Learned optimism: How to change your mind and your life.* New York: Pocket Books.

Seligman, M. E. P. (1993). *What you can change . . . and what you can't: The complete guide to successful self-improvement.* New York: Ballantine Books.

Seligman, M. E. P. (2002). *Authentic happiness: Using the new positive psychology to realize your potential for lasting fulfillment.* New York: Free Press.

Selye, H. (1974). *Stress without distress.* Philadelphia: J. B. Lippincott, Co.

Sexton, L. (1999). Vicarious traumatisation of counsellors and effects on their workplaces. *British Journal of Guidance & Counselling, 27,* 393–403.

Shea, S. B. (2004). Mind over meltdown. *Natural Health, 34,* 68.

Shelton, L., & Horne, N. (2004). Strong, serene and centered: Take a stand against stress with this anxiety-busting, resilience-building strength workout. *Natural Health, 34*, 88.

Sherman, M. D. (1996). Distress and professional impairment due to mental health problems among psychotherapists. *Clinical Psychology Review, 16*, 299–315.

Simon, C. E., Pryce, J. G., Roff, L. L., & Klemmack, D. (2005). Secondary traumatic stress and oncology social work: Protecting compassion from fatigue and compromising the worker's worldview. *Journal of Psychosocial Oncology, 23*, 1–14.

Skovolt, T. M. (2001). *The resilient practitioner: Burnout prevention and self-care strategies for counselors, therapists, teachers, and health professionals.* Boston: Allyn & Bacon.

Skovholt, T. M., Grier, T. L., & Hanson, M. R. (2001). Career counseling for longevity: Self-care and burnout prevention strategies for counselor resilience. *Journal of Career Development, 27*(3), 167–176.

Snyder, C. R., & Lopez, S. J. (Eds.). (2002). *Handbook of positive psychology.* Oxford: Oxford University Press.

Sowa, C. J., & May, K. M. (1994). Occupational stress within the counseling profession: Implications for counselor training. *Counselor Education & Supervision, 34*(1), 19–30.

Spicuzza, F. J., & de Voe, M. W. (1982). Burnout in the helping professions: Mutual aid groups as self-help. *Personnel and Guidance Journal, 61*, 95–99.

Stern, D. (2004). *The present moment in psychotherapy and everyday life.* New York: W. W. Norton & Co.

Storr, A. (1988). *On solitude.* New York: Bantam.

Strand, C. (1988). *The wooden bowl.* New York: Hyperion.

Strumpfer, D. J. (2003). Resilience and burnout: A stitch that could save nine. *South African Journal of Psychology, 33*, 69–79.

Sussman, M. B. (1992). *A curious calling: Unconscious motivations for practicing psychotherapy.* Northvale, NJ: Jason Aronson.

Selected Bibliography

Suzuki, S. (1973). *Zen mind, beginner's mind.* New York: John Weatherhill.

Tugade, M. M., & Fredrickson, B. L. (2004). Resilient individuals use positive emotions to bounce back from negative emotional experiences. *Journal of Personality and Social Psychology, 86,* 320–333.

Tusaie, K., & Dyer, J. (2004). Resilience: A historical review of the construct. *Holistic Nursing Practice, 18,* 3–10.

Ungar, M., Mackey, L., Guest, M., & Bernard, C. (2000). Logotherapeutic guidelines for therapists' self-care. *International Forum for Logotherapy, 23,* 89–94.

Valente, V., & Marotta, A. (2005). The impact of yoga on the professional and personal life of the psychotherapist. *Comtemporary Family Therapy, 27*(1), 65–80.

Vandecreek, L., & Allen, J. B. (Eds.). (2005). *Innovations in clinical practice: Focus on health and wellness.* Sarasota, FL: Professional Resource Press.

VanMeter, J. B., McMinn, M. R., Bissell, L. D., Kaur, M., & Pressley, J. D. (2001). Solitude, silence, and the training of psychotherapists: A preliminary study. *Journal of Psychology and Theology, 29,* 22–28.

Walsh, S., & Cormack, M. (1994). "Do as we say but not as we do": Organizational, professional and personal barriers to the receipt of support at work. *Clinical Psychology and Psychotherapy, 1,* 101–110.

Walsh, R., & Shapiro, S. L. (2006). The meeting of meditative disciplines and western psychology: A mutually enriching dialogue. *American Psychologist, 61,* 227–239.

Warner, C. (1992). *The last word: A treasury of women's quotes.* Englewood Cliffs, NJ: Prentice Hall Trade.

Watkins, Jr., C. E. (1983). Burnout in counseling practice: Some potential professional and personal hazards of becoming a counselor. *Personnel and Guidance Journal, 61,* 304–308.

Weiss, A. (2004). *Beginning mindfulness: Learning the way of awareness.* Novato, CA: New World Library.

Weiss, L. (2004). *Therapist's guide to self-care.* New York: Routledge/ Taylor & Francis.

Wicks, R. (1986). *Availability.* New York: Crossroad.

Wicks, R. (1988). *Living simply in an anxious world.* Mahwah, NJ: Paulist Press.

Wicks, R. (1992). *Touching the holy.* Notre Dame: Ave Maria Press.

Wicks, R. (1995). The stress of spiritual ministry: Practical suggestions on avoiding unnecessary distress. In R. Wicks (Ed.), *Handbook of spirituality for ministers: Vol. 1* (pp. 249–258). Mahwah, NJ: Paulist Press.

Wicks, R. (1997). *After 50: Spiritually embracing your own wisdom years.* New York: Paulist Press.

Wicks, R. (1998). *Living a gentle, passionate life.* Mahwah, NJ: Paulist Press.

Wicks, R. (2000). *Simple changes.* Notre Dame: Thomas More/Sorin Books.

Wicks, R. (2002). *Riding the dragon.* Notre Dame: Sorin Books.

Wicks, R. (2003). Countertransference and burnout in pastoral counseling. In R. Wicks, R. Parsons, & D. Capps (Eds.), *Clinical handbook of pastoral counseling: Vol. 3* (pp. 321–341). Mahwah, NJ: Paulist Press.

Wicks, R. (2006). *Overcoming secondary stress in medical and nursing practice: A guide to professional resilience and personal well-being.* New York : Oxford University Press.

Wicks, R., & Hamma, R. (1996). *Circle of friends: Encountering the caring voices in your life.* Notre Dame: Ave Maria Press.

Williams, E., Konrad, T., Scheckler, W., Pathman, D., Linzer, M., McMurray, J., et al. (2001). Understanding physicians' intentions to withdraw from practice: The role of job satisfaction, job stress, and mental and physical health. *Health Care Management Review, 26,* 7–19.

Zaslove, M. (2001). American Academy of Family Physicians. *Curbside consultation: A case of physician burnout.* American Family Physician. Available at http://www.aafp.org/afp/2001/08/01/curbside.html.

Zunz, S. J. (1998). Resiliency and burnout: Protective factors for human service managers. *Administration in Social Work, 22,* 39–54.

Permissions

I am grateful for the following permissions to use previously copyrighted material:

Excerpts from *Riding the Dragon* by Robert J. Wicks, © 2003. Used by permission of the publisher, Sorin Books, an imprint of Ave Maria Press Inc., P. O. Box 428, Notre Dame, IN, 46556, www.avemariapress. com. Used with permission of the publisher.

Excerpts from *Simple Changes* by Robert J. Wicks, © 2000. Used by permission of the publisher, Thomas More Publishing, an imprint of Ave Maria Press Inc., P.O. Box 428, Notre Dame, IN, 46556, www.ave mariapress.com.

Excerpts from *Touching the Holy* by Robert J. Wicks, © 1992 by Ave Maria Press, P.O. Box 428, Notre Dame, IN, 46556, www.avemariapress.com.

Excerpts from *Clinical Handbook of Pastoral Counseling: Vol. 3*, edited by Robert J. Wicks, D. Parsons, and D. Capps, © 2003, Paulist Press, Inc., Mahwah, NJ, www.paulistpress.com. Used with permission of Paulist Press.

Excerpts from *Handbook of Spirituality for Ministers: Vol. 1*, edited by Robert J. Wicks, © 1995, Paulist Press, Inc., Mahwah, NJ, www. paulistpress.com. Used with permission of Paulist Press.

Permissions

Excerpts from *Living a Gentle, Passionate Life* by Robert J. Wicks, © 1998, Paulist Press, Inc., Mahwah, NJ, www.paulistpress.com. Used with permission of Paulist Press.

Excerpts from *Living Simply in an Anxious World* by Robert J. Wicks, © 1988, Paulist Press, Inc., Mahwah, NJ, www.paulistpress.com. Used with permission of Paulist Press.

Excerpts from *After 50: Spiritually Embracing Your Own Wisdom Years* by Robert J. Wicks, © 1997, Paulist Press, Inc., Mahwah, NJ, www.paulist press.com. Used with permission of Paulist Press.

Excerpts from *Overcoming Secondary Stress in Medical and Nursing Practice* by Robert J. Wicks, © 2006, Oxford University Press, New York, www.oup.com. Used with permission of Oxford University Press.

Excerpts from *On Being a Therapist* by Jeffrey A. Kottler, © 1989, Jossey-Bass Publishers, San Francisco. Used with permission of Jossey-Bass Publishers.

Excerpts from *Caring for Ourselves: A Therapist's Guide to Personal and Professional Well-Being* by Ellen K. Baker, © 2003, American Psychological Association. Used with the author's permission.

Index

Index